How To Manifest Like A God

Like A God

Lorae Knight

DEDICATION

To my dearest daughter. You are the light which
grounds me. Thank you for everything.

CONTENTS

ACKNOWLEDGMENTS

I remain in eternal gratitude to the omnipotent spirit flowing through all things. Through its gift of unconditional love, I have been graced with the vision, teachers and wisdom that brought along with it the words written here. I extended great gratitude to many gurus and mentors who have shared their knowledge with humanity including Neville Goddard, Mooji, Sadguru, Brian Scott, Joseph Rodrigues, Abraham Hicks, Ram Dass, Earl Nightingale, Napoleon Hill, Bob Proctor, Paulo Coelho and many others who have inspired so many with their divine insight.

Thank you to all the light beings who have graced me with their love and stories. It is your journey that co-creates with mine and made it possible to bring this to other co-creators. I must also pay huge respect and gratitude to the individuals whose stories have been shared in this book and the authors of the religious texts whose words have been quoted. Their dedication to unfolding the truth of the omnipotent is what has enabled the relative truth of god in the human condition to be revealed here.

1 WHAT IS MANIFESTING?

Manifestation simply means to give tangible life to the things that you most want in the universe. You can manifest things in numerous ways, some of which I will outline in this book, but fundamentally the key principles to manifesting come from these three very simple statements: You attract what you are. You are what you think about the most. You move what you have attracted to you by doing. These three statements are important for the student of manifesting to inherit. It must also be understood that these three statements are governed by supreme laws which take precedence over the natural and the spiritual world. Many of these laws will be revealed as you journey through these pages but one of the fundamental laws which you should first understand before going any further on your quest for love, peace and riches is this: Everything in this universe is made up of some kind of energy, this includes yourself. When you learn to manipulate energy in such a way that it serves your conscious desires, you can claim yourself to be a master manifester. In the words printed here, you will be exposed to the master's work. You will gain great insight into the tools, practices and mindsets shared with mankind by individuals who have mastered these energies in such a way that they have come to be considered gods. Through the total embodiment of the concepts herein, the individuals who you will learn about became magnets for their deepest desires and a portal for supreme laws to work through. Each one of the individuals who reside in this book was born as a mere mortal. This should encourage you to know that if you are also a mere mortal, you possess all the capabilities needed to reach a god level of manifestation mastery. Simply by embracing the concepts in the following chapters, you will learn how to live your life in such a way that opportunities, people, places and things that correlate to your highest state will begin moving effortlessly towards you. The movement at first may be slow and subtle but as you begin to build momentum and become a true master, the world around you will bow to your every command. A common concept you may be aware of when thinking about manifesting is the law of attraction. This is the belief that our thoughts are responsible for what we create and who we become. Positive thoughts lead to positive situations and negative thoughts lead to negative situations.

Our thoughts are a huge component when it comes to manifesting, so much so that an entire chapter has been dedicated to understanding them. For some time now the law of attraction, based on the concept of thoughts, has been making its way into the mainstream mind. It has been termed as a secret sorcery to success used mostly by the elites to dominate the world. Many of the world's elites indeed use mastery techniques to get to where they are today, but for anyone who is to be in control of the circumstances in their life, the law of attraction is a paramount concept to master. In this book, we will venture a little deeper and beyond the concept of the law of attraction. We will look at various types of energies that live within us which for many have been left dormant and sleeping covertly in our times of need. As you read on through the words written here, you will gradually awaken those hidden energies by learning tools and practical examples of how to harness them. Some of the messages may not come to you as easily as the others but do not be disheartened. Continue to read what has been expressed and learn from the divine beings who manifested their dreams through the use of these lessons.

Mastering how to be the god of your very own universe will not resonate with everyone in this lifetime. It will require, in most cases, a complete paradigm shift and also the need to let go of certain things, people and thoughts which keep us in bondage to the way that things have always been. Becoming a master manifester begins with our mindset. We must first believe that we do indeed have the power within us to create and manifest anything that our heart truly desires. We must also recognise that we have full responsibility for the way that our life currently is and for the way our life will be in the future.

To assume responsibility and sovereignty over one's own life requires extreme courage, a courage which is becoming rarer in this 21st century. To become a master manifester, you must first stop blaming the government, your parents, the country you were born in, the bullies at school/work or any other external excuse as to why you can not have what it is that you desire the most. You can have anything that you desire. Anything. However, if you have any doubt, excuses or something to transfer responsibility for your circumstance over to anything but yourself, you will not have any success as a master manifester. If you are not able to assume complete responsibility for everything that has occurred in your life and will occur, then what has been written here will not work for you. This is law.

Another thing to mention before we dive deep into this is that you must exert maximal willpower to bring about the desired state that floods your dreams. This is especially true if the manifestation is 'far out' from the current belief systems and surrounding environment that you currently have. When things inevitably get tough. When it seems that your dreams are too ambitious to ever become true, the only thing which will defeat these enemies of progress is the will to bring about the desired manifestation. Patience will be a strong ally to willpower on your journey to becoming a master manifester.

As you will learn as you follow my words, manifesting is not instantaneous in the 3D realm. There are certain cycles, ebbs and flows that energy must pass through before it can be transformed into a new desired state. Because of this, it is important to be in recognition of your becoming. Enjoy the journey because this life is not only about reaching our final destination. The true beauty of life lies in your gradual progression towards the desired manifestation. There will be times in life when things appear to be falling apart, especially if you have not begun the master's work. In these times, the master manifester will deliberately see things as falling together because they have faith in their manifesting abilities and the teachings laid out in these pages.

I will finish this introduction to manifesting with this: As far as we know, we only have this one life. We do not know when our time is up and we do not know what will happen to us when this life comes to an end. We do know however that we are alive now. We assume that by the grace of the omnipotent god power that tomorrow, we will be alive again. We do not know what tomorrow will bring but what if we did know? What if we could choose exactly what our day would look like tomorrow. What would you dream of doing and who would you dream of becoming if you knew that you only had tomorrow and that you could live tomorrow in any way that you pleased? What would you do today to make that dream of tomorrow become today's reality? Most people don't realise their uttermost dreams because they do not dream big enough or they do not believe it is possible. Do not limit yourself for your imagination is limitless and whatever you can imagine you can become.

One of my favourite writers is Paulo Coelho, author of The Alchemist. The Alchemist is filled with quotations, teachings and pointings which can accompany a master manifester on their journey to becoming. Significant takeaways from his book are the four obstacles that the author notes are the barriers as to why one may never realise their dreams. They are described as follows.

1. *"We learn from childhood onwards that everything we want to do is impossible. There comes a time when our personal calling is so deeply buried in our soul it becomes almost invisible."*

The voices of our parents, peers and pressures from society ring frequently in our minds, discouraging us from becoming what is truly in our hearts to become. As a student of mastering manifestation, you must learn to drown out the noise, the doubters and naysayers. Do not let their fears project onto you. Stand firm in your heart and trust in the power that created everything.

2. *"We know what we want to do, but are afraid of hurting those around us by abandoning everything in order to pursue our dream."*

When pursuing your most desired manifestations you must learn to enter a mode of engaged detachment. We become so attached to those we love and the familiarity of doing things a certain way that we can sacrifice all our heart's desires in the name of love. True love is expansive and love wants to see you fulfil the highest version of yourself. It is not necessary to abandon your loved ones or shy away from responsibilities but it is your obligation to focus and visuals a dream which is harmonious to who you truly are and what you truly love.

3. *"Fear."*

It is often said that there are only two emotions: Love and Fear. Every other emotion lies within the spectrum of these two emotions, to some varying degree. Fear is one of the lowest vibrations/ energies in existence. It paralyses us and coerces us into doing things we do not truly want to do. It keeps us stagnant and cripples us from acting in the way we know we must act to realise our dreams. Do away with fear and treat it like a plague. Fear will inevitably appear on your journey to manifesting like a god, as it is a necessary human emotion. To overcome fear, hold onto the vision of the truest desire living within your heart for what you desire often lies on the other side of fear.

Finally 4. *"Fear of realising your dreams."*

Many of us fear realising our desires because we fear who we will become if we do. So many condemn the rich as if they are evil and the cheats of society. As a result of this mentality, many believe that if they were to become rich, they would be viewed in the same way. Others fear standing out from their crowd of family and friends they have grown up with for fear of 'outshining' them and so would rather live miserably so that they can fit in. What these people have not considered is the happiness, lessons and growth that come from pursuing your destiny. Life will come and go whatever you choose to do. There will be hard times and good times regardless of your success however you will live a much more satisfying life if you choose to live one which gratifies the burning desires of your heart.

Although a fictional character, I would like to carry on the theme here from Paulo Coelho's The Alchemist and tell you about a merchant who gave up on pursuing his dreams.

The merchant had owned his crystal shop for over 30 years. He was a devoted Muslim and as a young man had dreamed of fulfilling his desire of travelling from Morocco to Mecca.

As a young man, he had worked hard to save up for his crystal shop and vowed that he would travel to Mecca just as soon as he had enough money to do so. The years went by and the shop kept nicely afloat, affording the merchant a pretty decent lifestyle. Every year the merchant would watch pilgrims on their journey to Mecca, some with tremendous wealth but most poorer than he. Every year he watched others realise his one true wish and every year he did nothing to make his truest desire a reality.

On one unexpected day, a young boy from Spain entered his shop. Barely speaking a word of Arabic, the boy asked the merchant for a job. Seeing that the boy was clearly in need, the merchant offered him some wages to clean the crystals and a commission for any crystals he sold. The boy got to work right away with zeal and enthusiasm. He polished the shop every day from top to bottom and always made sure that every customer left with a smile. The business began to pick up for the merchant's crystal shop and soon the boy learnt more and more Arabic.

The merchant learned that the boy was in pursuit of a destiny following a dream of travelling to the pyramids. Although the boy was humble and honest, the merchant suspected that there was another unrevealed reason for his adventures. The merchant learned that the boy was once a shepherd but had lost the wealth of his flock to a thief. As many do, the merchant began to discourage the boy's dreams. He deemed the journey to the pyramids pointless and minimised one of the wonders of the world by condemning the pyramids to a mere pile of rocks. The boy replied to the merchant that he wouldn't understand why he wanted to go to the pyramids because he was not a dreamer like himself. This made the merchant think sadly about his failure to realise his dream of travelling to Mecca. He realised that his failure was the only reason he was discouraging the boy from pursuing his destiny.

The time came, almost a year after they had first met, that the boy had finally recovered his losses from the thief. He now had enough money to buy twice as many sheep as he originally had if he so chose. The boy knew that he had fulfilled what he had come to do at the merchant's shop and recognised it was time to move on to the next part of his journey. He told the Merchant that he was going home to his sheep but the merchant knew that what he spoke was not true. He disclosed to the boy that the difference between them was that the boy was on the way to making his dreams come true whereas he, the merchant, simply dreamed about pursuing his truest desires but had no willpower to do anything about it. It was the dream of becoming that kept him going, day in and day out at the shop. The boy had brought much success to the shop, success which the merchant feared because he knew that it would require him to upgrade and change his lifestyle. The merchant was in fear of change and was comfortable living the way that he had always lived for the last thirty years. The boy had been an inspiration for him and he learned something about himself; that he was comfortable being just comfortable and that he would rather dream about his dream rather than actually make it happen and for him that was okay.

If you want to be like the merchant, comfortable with the way your life is and fearful of change then this might be the end of this journey for you at this time. If however, you hear the siren's call to attract all the magnificent abundance and love that this life has to offer, let go of fear, embrace love and let us begin the journey.

2 MEDITATION

Even with the continuous traffic of activity, distractions and chaos we face day to day, please know that there is a peaceful place within you. This place is subtle, silent and carries a magnitude of manifesting power. Within this place resides all the desires and secrets known and unknown to man. You can go to this place at any time you like, although it is often easier to find it when you are alone and resting. Some of the best times to practice manifesting within this place of peace come just before going to bed or first thing when you rise up from sleep. The best way you can become the observer of this inner sanctuary is through the technique of meditation. If you have never meditated before, fear not. I am going to share with you some potent techniques for you to become the space of eternal nothingness which resides inside every being. But first, let me explain what the purpose of meditation is.

I'm sure you've heard many times that each one of us comes into this world as a blank canvas. Soon after, our emptiness is filled by daily Pavlovian programming until we eventually become the person who we believe we are today. This is true to some extent. Yes, we do come into the world free beings with little to no attachments but we also come into the world in the human condition. To be born as a human means we are automatically bound to the limitations of our meandering mind and bulky body. So no, unfortunately, we do not enter this world free to be the pure soul which is our natural state of being. Instead, we grow and are given a name, and a diet, along with a mother and a father. We are told what we can do and what we can't do. We are told what is for us and what is not for us. Someone tells us what to wear, how to behave, what our future should look like etc, etc.

It is this 'programming' from the outside world which makes you into a person. When this person's name is called, you automatically begin to act out all the programmes associated with this individual's personality. This character is not your true self. Your true self is the endless quiet that quaintly lingers in the ether; waiting for you, the character, to pay attention to it. Now if you have never meditated before, you may never have met your true self or at least not for a long time. This is okay however, it is important to note that your true self, is always with you. Your true self can be described as a state of contented bliss and it is not something you can find by searching for it. The only way to find your true self is by removing your character's programming and attachments so that you can simply be your true self.

Why is any of this important? Well, it is from this subtle source of bliss that you harness your natural ability to manifest your desired life. It is here in the ethereal emptiness where all and nothing is written. It is also here, in your subtle silence, that you possess the power of ultimate creation and timelessness. Your awareness or lack of awareness of its existence should tell you that it is not something that you can fully become. If you were to fully become the pure empty self you would cease to exist in this reality as the individual you know yourself to be. Instead, your spirit would live on within all things for eternity, as you will come to find out one day. If you are on a spiritual journey to know yourself and have not come to this recognition, please do not be discouraged by my words. We have been blessed with techniques like sitting with 'the silence' so that we may know the nature of the true internal self. In contrast, we have been given this human mind and human body so that we may create an external reality that is most pleasing to our higher self.

Earl Nightingale once said: *"We are all self-made but only the successful will admit it."*

And he is right. Whether we like to admit it or not, each one of us has tuned ourselves to a frequency that reflects the life that we are living today. The life that we see in the present moment is due to the frequency we were tuned to in the past. The circumstance that we will live through in the future is a direct result of the frequency that we are creating in this moment. See it like this: When you first get into a car and you switch on the radio, it doesn't automatically play the station that you like. You have to first turn the dial and find the transmitting frequency which best resonates with how you are feeling that day. If you are going to the gym maybe you want to listen to some house music. If you are driving home to see a loved one, maybe you want to listen to some Jazz or R&B. Whatever it is that you wish to listen to, you don't just get it straight away simply because you want it. You first have to tune yourself to the frequency of it. This is true for all of our lives. To do what you want to do and be who you want to be first, you must find the frequency of it and then you become it.

The problem is so many of us are already living with dozens of tunings and programmes which we did not choose and are not a true reflection of our higher self. It is not your fault that you have some of these programs, especially those installed in us from early childhood. It is however your responsibility as an adult to transmute, transform and turn off the programmes that do not serve you. This requires some basic knowledge of self and a lot of deep diving into your eternal being. I do not expect you to discover who you are, why you are the way you are and what your purpose in life is simply from reading this book. Soul searching requires a lot of self-recognition, self-enquiry, light-work and shadow-work. (Don't worry shadow work is not some sort of voodoo, it simply means to reveal and play out the programmes of ourselves that we hide usually because they are related to traumas.) By using meditation as a daily tool, you can begin to use it to have a few moments in your day where you can 'escape' the programming and just allow yourself to be your true self. You will instantly know you are being your true self because you will reside in a state of perfect peace, bountiful bliss and calming contentment. Once you are in this blank canvas space, you can reprogramme your mind by visualising scenes and listening to words that affirm the frequency that you wish to be on. For example, you may visualise your bank account with a positive balance of seven figures. You may choose to see yourself in the loving embrace of a loved one, dancing on a soft sandy beach out in the Bahamas. You can also repeat mantras or affirmations to yourself over and over again in your meditations so that your subconscious mind becomes aware of the lifestyle you are creating. Once your subconscious mind knows of the future you are intentionally creating, it begins to subtly move you in the direction to bring those desires to hand. I am aware that you will not be able to effectively meditate while your eyes are fixated on reading these words, however, illustrated below is a simple technique that you can do straight after reading this which will help you to find that state of bliss. In addition, I have inserted a link to a youtube video where you can find a guided meditation for you to enjoy for free!

https://youtu.be/WLTaZBLS78c

The meditation relates directly to the technique that I have described here.

First of all, find a quiet place. You can do this any time of the day however between 03:00-06:00 am is a very energetically effective time to meditate. This is because the electromagnetic field of the earth returns to the horizon and brings with it mystical magic. Your mind is also well-rested and free from pretty much all thoughts and feelings at this time. Many people also like to meditate in the evenings, when all their tasks have been done and their mind is ready to relax. It is crucial that you relax. Once you have found a quiet, relaxing place, lay down flat with your spine happily horizontal. You may also choose to sit in a comfortable armchair or a lotus position. Honestly, unless you are playing with energy poses, it does not matter how you position yourself. The main thing is to be comfortable.

Once you feel calm, close your eyes. Your eyes will remain closed for the duration of the meditation. With your eyes closed, take a deep, slow, expansive breath in. Let your lungs be generously filled with air. If you like you can count up to 8 while filling up your lungs. Once your breath is at full capacity, breathe out slowly for a count of four. While you are breathing out, hum the sound 'Om'. Let the sound of Om come out from your lungs and be carried through to every cell in your body. Do this slowly and as loudly or as quietly as you feel comfortable with. You should feel the 'Om' end at the centre of your body, known as the Solar Plexus. (The Solar Plexus is located in a vortex behind your stomach and is the chakra related to your personal power.) Repeat this 3 times. Your body should feel completely relaxed and you will begin to feel yourself enter a state of bliss. The reason we use 'Om' is that it is the first sound ever to exist and all creation came from it. Its vibration alone transports us to a place of pure self while relaxing every cell in the body instantaneously.

Continue the slow, deep breathing throughout the meditation but don't force the rhythm. Find your flow and allow your sense of self to sink into this peaceful pace by breathing in and breathing out. Breathing in and breathing out. Focus your attention on your breath for a moment. Watch how your chest rises and falls effortlessly; like the waves of the ocean gently brushing the sand on the shore, before returning to the deep infinite waters. Breathe in and out, chest up and down. Just observe how you breathe for a moment. While you are observing your breath, you may also feel a faint trickle of air on your upper lip. Slow everything down and allow your body to breathe for you effortlessly.

You may also feel your heart pumping away peacefully in your chest. Watch its faithful tempo supporting your life. It beats all by itself, yet there is a subtle force behind it. What is this force which keeps your heart beating? Who is this force? Who in this moment is observing the force that keeps your heart in tempo? Stay here for a moment. Be still and at peace, just watching the state of your being.

If any distracting thoughts pop into your mind; such as what you are going to do after this meditation or what happened to you earlier today, just allow them to come in but don't touch them. Just observe them in the same way you have been observing your breath. Just as the air filling up your chest flows in and then peacefully flows out, allow your thoughts to flow into your mind and then flow out without touching them. Be here, in peace now. There is plenty of time to think about what you have to do later and stress about the things not serving you but right now you are here, as your true self. Peace. Bliss and contentment.

Now you have found your emptiness and this emptiness is you. Free of attachments, free of needs and desires. Ask yourself, what do I need at this moment? A few things may pop into your mind but just observe them like you have been observing your breath. Where are these desires coming from, if any? Are they in the same place as the force that is pacing your heart or are they coming from your programmes? Observe them. What you will soon come to realise is in this place as your true self, there are no needs. Any longings that are placed in your mind or body are only wants. As your true self, you don't need anything. Indeed, you may have felt your breathing slow all the way down; as if you do not even need to breathe, only you want to breathe. You want to live life here on earth and you realise that you already have all that you need to live in peace, bliss and contentment. Anything your mind or body desires are just wants, not needs but through manifestation mastery you may have them all. The force pulsing in your heart is the force that will bring all your wants to you, so that you may enjoy them in this life.

Observe the beating of your heart. Become familiar with the force behind its rhythm. Breathe in, Breathe out. This is the god force in you. The unfailing beating is a physical manifestation of the god force's unconditional love. It resides in you. It is you. Now while you are in a completely peaceful state, with your attention on your heart, picture an orb of green or pink light glowing around your heart. Each time you feel your heart pulse, imagine that the glowing light is growing bigger and bigger. It starts to illuminate your chest and your neck, your face and your arms. Still, the light grows with each beat of your heart. Now it has reached the base of your belly and is expanding outwards beyond your body as it reaches down your legs. Your body is now fully encased in this green glow and with each heartbeat it grows bigger, filling up the room you are laying in. As you observe the light expanding, you see it fill every corner of your home and the building itself. With each beat of your heart, it grows. You can see the glow extending all over the city that you live in. It shines now all through the globe and out into the expansive atmosphere. The source of this green glow is still within your beating heart. You are now a magnet for manifestation. With this green light surrounding your reality, only the things which you desire, which are born out of unconditional love can come to you.

Picture yourself wearing the clothes you wish to wear. What do they feel like? How many layers do you have on? What colour are they? Picture every detail from your headwear to your shirt all down to your shoes. Put in every minuscule detail and feel yourself dressed in your desires. While you are here in these wonderful, luxurious clothes, feel the pulse of your heart drumming in every cell of your body. Every part of your body where you can feel the pulse of your heart is radiating the green magnetic glow. The magnetic green aura is attracting the clothing of your desire to you now.

Now, still wearing these magnificent garments, turn your attention to your ears. Watch how your ears become sensitive and alert as you put your attention to them. Feel each cell in your ear radiating with the rhythm of your heartbeat. Listen to the joy, laughter and friendly chatter flooding your ears. Can you feel how the joy fills up your being as you listen to the happiness? Who is laughing like that? Can you hear the specific voices of people you love or the people you wish to be associated with? You are the source of their joy. Listen for as long as you need.

Pay attention now to the sound of the sea. Listen to how peaceful the waves crash onto the shore. As the distant song of sea birds reaches you, their loving call makes the radiant rhythm in your heart glow with even more intensity. Feel how thankful you are to be here right now. Look around in your mind's eye. What can you see? Are you still wearing the beautiful clothes your heart desires you to wear? Who is with you? Maybe a loved one who is also dressed just as lavishly as you. They have a grand smile on their face which radiates with the love that you have glowing from your heart. Breathe in, breathe out.

Look to the left of you and picture a large, long table adorned with your favourite food and drink. Every inch of the table is covered with your favourite meals, desserts and appetisers, all of them handmade by your favourite chef. Can you smell the bountiful banquet? What kind of smells are there? Taste the sweetness of tropical, tantalizing fruits grace your pallet. Savour the savoury snacks that make you salivate. Indulge in the delicious desserts that delightfully fill your plenty. There are one hundred and fifty chairs at the banquet and each seat is filled by an individual who you love or admire. Who is there? See their faces and look each individual in their eyes. Take your time doing this but do not make it an effort. Breathe in, breathe out.

Look to the right of you. There in your mind's eye stands the most spectacular architect. It is your home. What does it look like? What materials is it made of? Wood, brick or a natural landscape? How many rooms are there? Is there a pool or a natural stream? Look at how the space expands all around you. All that you can hold in your vision belongs to you. Your dream car is parked on the driveway and the keys are in your pocket. Can you feel them in there? There are beautiful, exotic flowers complimenting the breathtaking view that your home possesses. Feel in your heart the great sense of satisfaction and gratitude you have now knowing that you have just manifested your dream home and lifestyle. Walk up the path to your home, take the keys out of your pocket and open the door. Embrace the luxury and gifts from distant lands that reside in your residence, just for a moment. Smile. Now make your way to your bedroom or a comfortable area of your home. While you are making your way there, awe the inspiring views which paint every window in your home. As you enter your room, see everything that brings you comfort there. Find your bed with beautiful satin sheets and lay down right where you are. You are here now, laying down in your room. Feel your heart beating with satisfaction. Stay here for a moment, delighting in the satisfaction. Feel gratitude wash all over your being. Now focus your attention again on your breathing, moving your chest slowly up and down. Gradually open your eyes and return to your space.

That's the end of the meditation. Take some time to be in the present moment. There is no need to jump up and start any activity. Remember your true self has no desire to do anything but be. You have plenty of time to 'do' in another moment but in this moment just be with yourself. Slowly regain your named self but this time you have a peaceful mind because you know bliss and abundance are just a meditation away.

Meditation has come into the western world in the last century or so and can be traced back to the east for many millennia. Among those famous for popularising meditation is Buddha. In 563 BC, Siddhartha Gautama was born to a noble emperor of an intricate state. Before his birth,

Gautama's mother dreamt of a white elephant, garnished in splendid dress, entering her womb. Gautama's mother delivered him naturally and with ease, by leaning up against a tree with two doulas to support her. Lotus flowers began to bloom where he was born which guided a wise oracle to make a prophecy about the newborn's destiny.
He prophesied that Gautama would become a great ruler of many nations or that he was to be the most powerful sage that history had ever known.

His father, being of noble stature, aspired for his son to become an exalted emperor and so vowed that he would keep his son sheltered from yogis so that he would not be enticed by their teachings. He also kept his son from knowing any form of suffering so that he would have no desire for religion.

And so the emperor's promise was upheld. From birth until coming of age, Gautama was showered with rare riches and plenty of pleasures. Every day there were banquets, music and dancing. Gautama lived a life of luxury and every wish he desired was granted to him. Whether practising martial arts by some of the greatest masters or being entertained in the palace by famous actors, for Gautama, there was never a dull day in the kingdom. When he was of age, Gautama was wed to a beautiful young princess and soon she had borne him a son named Rāhula. Gautama's life was all that a prince could ask for, but although suffering and religion could be kept from entering the palace, the winds of destiny could not.

One day, while out on a routine ride, Gautama became curious as to what lay beyond the familiar places of his kingdom. He commanded his charioteer that they take a solo trip into the city so that he may satisfy his curiosity. As they made their way through the busy city, something caught Gautama's attention. Something he had never seen before. It was an old woman, as ancient as the Baobab tree. The aged woman folded over her walking stick as she struggled to stay upright. Her steps were as slow as a giant tortoise and as delicate as a feather made of porcelain. The pampered prince, utterly perplexed, turned to his charioteer and asked what was wrong with the aged woman. The charioteer explained that there was nothing wrong with the frail woman, she was simply old and that old age was the common destiny for all beings, including the prince. The news startled Gautama, which then turned to sorrow as he saw his own face on the frame of the elderly woman.

The two continued through the city and yet another foreign phenomenon met the eyes of Gautama. There, just inches from a gutter lay a man grey in colour and covered in sores and boils. Every so often the sick man would cough horrendously. His coughs were so violent that after each episode he would clasp his chest tightly and needle in as much air as was possible so that death would not take him. Gautama was horrified and turned again to his charioteer to ask what was wrong with the man. The charioteer replied nonchalantly that the man was simply sick and that it can happen to absolutely anyone, anyone including a prince. Gautama shuddered as he pictured himself covered in disease, hanging onto dear life by the tips of his fingers.

Just before leaving the city, another sight caught Gautama's eyes. He heard miserable wailing making its way past the river banks and to the water. It was a funeral procession. The family of the deceased agonised as they carried the dead body on their shoulders and despair decorated their faces. Gautama felt their sorrow deep in his heart and once more turned to the charioteer for answers. The charioteer replied that the man they were carrying had come to the end of his days and that this was a certain prophecy for every person on earth, including the prince.

Gautama remained silent for the rest of the journey. What he had seen in the city haunted him; for he had never seen such misfortunes in all of his lean years. He realised he had been living in a fantasy and deemed his life meaningless. How could he ever be satisfied with his life of pleasures when he now knew that old age, sickness and death were a fate destined for all including himself. For several months Gautama remained disturbed by the scenes he had seen in the city and his life in the palace no longer satisfied him. He had everything, the riches, the glamorous wife and the male successor; however knowing the truth about life and the perishable impermanence of existence, Gautama felt as though he had nothing.

One night, depression overtook his reasoning and just like a thief in the night, Gautama slipped out of the palace and set off into the wilderness leaving everything and everyone behind. He vowed to himself that he would not return to the palace until he had found the ultimate truth and he would do whatever it took to know this. Consequently, his journey began.

Gautama replaced his royal robes with simple cloth. He shaved his hair for a fresh start and began his pursuit of enlightenment. In his first years as a spiritual student, he joined several meditation schools called Samadhis, eight to be exact. He sat with great meditation masters who taught Gautama various methods of transcending the mind and how to reach the place of oneness. Gautama spent many years in practice and although his teachers deemed him masterful in his meditations, it was not enough for him. Gautama had learned to stay in a state of bliss and contentment through meditation. He had learned how to detach from the physical world for hours and days on end however once he broke the meditation, like all practitioners, he found himself back in his usual mind-body suffering which he simply could not stand. Gautama longed for a permanent solution to overcome the impermanence of the physical world. And so Gautama bid farewell to his teachers and continued his journey to unveil the ultimate truth.

Gautama ventured into the forest where he had gone to be in isolation. While there, he came across a group of spiritual wanderers named the Samanas. They were frail and feral in appearance but their aura attracted Gautama to them. The Samana explained to Gautama that their spiritual practice meant that they did not go in pursuit of food. By ignoring their bodily desires, they could escape its hold against their being to act in ways that heed to its satisfaction. The Samana would sometimes be offered food from people in the towns they would pass through, kind people who were sensitive to their practice, but it was not their purpose to seek out bodily desires. Gautama, still in the search of truth, joined the ways of the Samanas and became just as frail and just as detached from worldly desires as them. For at least six years Gautama abstained from eating and dwelled in woodland areas where he was sometimes mistaken for a forest spirit by those bringing offerings from the towns nearby. He soon grew a following of disciples who were in awe of his radical ways.

One day Gautama was making his way through the wilderness to visit a nearby village. He came to a shallow river whose current was softly streaming along the banks. Gautama mustered up all the strength available in his body to make it across the river. When he was about halfway across, Gautama realised that he did not have the strength to continue. The meek river was stronger than he and its gentle current almost got the better of Gautama. He had to steady himself by holding onto a branch of a tree that lent its hand from the river's bank, or else he would have toppled over and drowned.

Gautama stayed here for some time. As he waded in the water, Gautama asked himself what it was that he had achieved in all these years. He had left his palace where everything he desired had been given to him. He had left his family, who he adored dearly. He had learned how to leave his mind through meditation and now how to leave his body so that it did not desire anything. Yet here he was, 2 degrees from death because of the torture he had put himself through but still he had not come to realise the ultimate truth.

Gautama crouched down to meet the river's water and revived himself in its purity. He made it to the other side of the river where his disciples gathered around him. They asked what he had discovered in the time he had spent holding onto the branch in the river. Gautama revealed that he had come to understand that the Samana practice would not bring one to enlightenment and asked his disciples to cook something for him to eat. His disciples were shocked by what he had to say and much losing faith in his divinity left him. One however did stay by his side, a milkmaid by the name of Sujātā. She offered him a bowl of rice pudding and after eating the hearty meal, Gautama regained his strength.

Gautama got up from the banks of the river and wandered over to rest under what is now known as a Bodhi tree. As he sat there, he deemed all his searching for the truth meaningless. He had lost so much and gained nothing. Even his disciples who had walked with him all these years believed he was not capable of achieving enlightenment. What was the meaning of this existence and would he ever discover its truth in this mind-body phenomena. Gautama sat under the tree and began to practice the meditation techniques he had learned right at the beginning of his journey to self-discovery. He vowed that he would not move from underneath the tree, nor would he break from meditation until he came to realise what it was that he had been searching for. If he should die there, underneath the Bodhi tree, then so be it.

For weeks Gautama sat under that Bodhi tree. The winds, the days and the nights came and went as they always did, watching Gautama vainly pursue his destiny. Then, on the first full moon of May, it happened. Gautama sat at the centre of his being and while in deep meditation, he removed himself from all his senses, attachments, urges and desires. He sat there at the very centre of it all and watched the turning wheel of life pivot around him. Never ceasing to stop, the wheel of life spun around him for an eternity. Everything in existence came to exist on that wheel and eventually came to end there also.

By the radiance of the moon, Gautama transcended his mind and became Buddha under what is now known as the Bodhi tree. Buddha means, the one who has transcended his mind. It was through meditation that Buddha transcended his mind and reached enlightenment. After many years of travelling and many years of abstaining from pursuing food, it was meditation that brought the great Buddha to a point of enlightenment. It was in the mind's eye where Buddha received the answer to all his striving and suffering. Through meditation, Buddha received what he desired most.

Buddha spent the rest of his life teaching across the land. Many of his teachings are written in the Dhammapada, guiding seekers of nirvana on their path. One of the first teachings talks about how we are our thoughts. We become the things that we think about. It is not always possible for us to control the traffic of thoughts that come into our minds moment by moment. You may have the full intention of thinking the best thoughts all day and then a bird defecates on you or you read an email that throws you off the entire day. Although we can not always control what happens in our day, we can control the images we put into our mind when we meditate. By practicing meditation we can re-tune our state of being and begin to feel and visualise the desires that we wish to manifest. A regular meditation practice can start to attract the places, people, objects and things you need in order to bring your manifestation to life. Not to mention it will also allow you to find the place in you that consists of pure eternal bliss. Never give this teaching up. Meditate as long as you want, but do not go long without meditation.

3 Tantric Sex

Every successful man or woman knows that the height of their success was significantly driven by a lover who ignited their sexual flame. Sex, or tantra, is a topic of conversation that we often giggle or blush over when mentioned in open conversation. It is however a topic we should be more open to talking about, especially as our manifested existence is a direct implication of two lovers performing the sacred act.

Every one of us has sexual urges. It feels good when we have the opportunity to have a meaningful intimate connection with another. It also feels good when we have the opportunity to release sexual energy which possesses an extreme creative power that none of us is talking about. Other than the fact that sex feels amazing, sexual desires can also be used as a tool for divine manifestation, when used correctly. Through tantric science, you can learn how to use the creative life force energy, generated during, sex to manifest your desired dream. This 'secret' of sex transmutation is widely known among those in possession of esoteric knowledge and has been practised throughout the ages. We will get into examples of pseudo goddesses who used tantra for manifestation later in the chapter but for now, let's get into the science of sex.

We are sentient beings living in an electromagnetic field. Sentient means that we can feel things through our five senses. An electromagnetic field is an electrical charge in motion, it is the force which gives all things a sense of life. To decipher the science of how we can manifest using sexual energy, it is important to understand the following analogy so listen closely.

You are an electromagnetic sentient being who is made up of two gender principles and two oppositely charged poles. As a sentient being, you possess a divine feminine principle and a divine masculine principle which come from your mother and father. As an electromagnetic being, you are made up of two charges: a positive charge and a negative charge, which come from divine life force energy. When you have sex, life force energy is created by the merging of two opposite poles. This is because the genitals of the male and the female are charged differently. A woman has a negative charge at her genitals and a positive charge at her heart. For a man, the opposite is true. He has a positive charge at his genitals and a negative charge at his heart. The positive charge is what we can call the pull energy. It is a call to attention, arousal and erection energy. The negative charge is the grounding energy, a place to plant seeds and allow things to ingest and grow.

When a woman is aroused, she is first called to action in the heart, at her positive charge. This gives way for her to be grounded and open at her negatively charged genitals, where a seed can be planted and grown.

When a man is aroused, he is first called to action in his genitals, which for him are positively charged. This gives way to grounding in his heart, where he can gain clarity and stability thus completing the circuit.

The generation of the life force energy in this way is so powerful that it can give birth to a whole other sentient being. However, it does not have to be only babies who are born out of the production of life force energy. We can also give birth to our desires and wishes when the life force energy is active. When life force energy is generated by the merging of two opposite poles, an infinite creative power infused with potentiality is activated. It is during this time of activation that there is potential to give birth to a new principle or desire in a timely efficient manner. To put this into perspective think about when a child is conceived. After conception, nothing more needs to be done for their physical manifestation. All bones, veins, personalities and genotypes are created within the womb of the feminine principle. The mother of the child and indeed the father needn't do anything more to bring about the existence of their child. This is the efficient power of sexual, life force energy. Once conception has taken place nothing more needs to be done but to wait for the arrival of the desire.

Although this is somewhat of an abstract concept to grasp, we know that in the physical realm it is true. We know that in the physical realm when two people of the opposite gender generate sexual energy a child is manifested within 9 months. How is it then true that if sexual energy is generated through the spiritual realm that a desire may be manifested after a period of conception? Let's dive a little deeper into the science.

You may or may not have heard of the magnetic and energetic invisible beams radiating from every being known as torus fields. Due to the masculine and feminine polarities of charge described above, we find ourselves obliviously walking around our everyday lives with an electromagnetic force field. This invisible force field is continuously attracting as well as pulling all things which are a vibrational match to us into our five sense reality.

To visualise what this invisible field looks like, imagine a doughnut. The doughnut can be whatever flavour you want so long as it is a torus shape with a hole in it. Visualise it floating in front of you with a bright beam of light rising up from the centre of the doughnut hole. Watch the light expanding out from the top and splitting into two separate beams, one beam curving to the left and the other curving to the right. Watch the light beams loop around the sides of the doughnut until they meet back at the base of the doughnut and rejoin at the centre as they make their way back through the hole.

This is literally what is happening to you at this very moment. A magnetic field is being generated in your heart, through the feminine principle and is being pushed from the heart right out of the top of your head by the masculine principle. It circles to the left and right of your body, down the sides of your arms and then comes back into the body through the base of the spine until it reaches the heart once more to complete the cycle. The magnetic field is being produced by the feminine principle and it attracts through the heart centre. The movement of this magnetic field is being driven by the masculine principle; the electricity which is influenced by the forces located at the genitals. You are a walking electromagnetic field of energy. You are a literal centre point of attraction with the ability to magnetise anything to you through the force of the feminine principle (the magnet). In contrast, through the masculine principle (electricity) you can physically pull those things towards you so that as a sentient being you can feel, touch, see, smell and taste all that you desire. Now that we understand the science, let's look at practical examples of how we can use the knowledge of gender, polarities and life force energy, generated through sex, to manifest our dream life.

We have all seen the glow that someone has when they are in love or have had a great night in the embrace of a lover. It is as if they have been supercharged with copious amounts of light to the point that they are beaming with high amounts of energy. You have to stop and ask yourself: "What in the world did that guy take, I want some of it too!" You can see them trying not to skip around the office or to hug every stranger that they meet on the street. It seems as if they can achieve anything they put their mind to and it would be right to assume this. This beaming is the power of life force energy which comes when a circuit of two polarities has been completed. If you are celibate or single don't worry, you can still achieve a circuit completion without having to engage in any physical sexual activities with another. You can still achieve the electromagnetic supercharge of life force energy without actually having to engage in physical sexual activities.

Let's review what we have learned so far. Firstly we know that we are made up of different principles: the divine feminine which is magnetic and the divine masculine which is electric. These parts make up an electromagnetic force field that surrounds your body and attracts to it things which match its frequency. We also know that the force field can be amped up through sexual, life force energy without a person having to engage in the act of physical sex. The reason that the life force energy can be generated in a being without having to engage in physical sex is that we all have both male and female principles residing within us. We also have a tool called the human imagination, which is an extremely powerful instrument in itself. By feeling through your imagination you can conjure up sexual life force energy and use it to give birth to your most desired manifestations. You can therefore trick your magnetic force field to charge itself up and attract what it is that you want to be born onto you. In the same sense, we can trick the electric field into grounding the magnetic energy so that we may plant the seed of desire into the infinite womb of wants and let it give birth to the things which we desire the most.

If you do have a lover who is open to energy work and wanted to try this technique together, then of course this is possible and can result in a truly divine and rapid manifestation. However, be very cautious. Energy work is not for the faint or impure of heart as we will discover later in the chapter. In addition, sex can result in pregnancy and must always be consensual. To do these techniques with a partner effectively, you must both be in sync with the desires of the heart. You must have a clear mind detached from fear and doubt. Your hearts and minds must be liberated from those things which you do not want to manifest. You must be sure that your partner's energy is clear and does not have any malice toward you also. Sexual energy is the purest and most sacred of energies besides unconditional love, therefore it should not be tampered with unless it is being used for the law of good and you know what you are doing. Okay, so now that the disclaimer is out of the way let's get into it.

Close your eyes. Okay now open them again because you have to read this next part to know what to do! No, but seriously, this technique can be done pretty much anywhere but it's best to be in a place where you are comfortable and won't be disturbed for a couple of moments. Maybe you're in your bed right now reading this or on a train with your earphones in. Maybe you are outside lounging on the grass. All of this is good. Just be sure that you feel relaxed and without haste to perform the technique. Now picture yourself within your mind's eye (that is the place between your two physical eyes) with the thing you desire the most.

What is in your hands while you are in the presence of the thing you desire? What does it feel like to touch those things? What can you smell? What can you see? Can you taste anything? What sounds are around you? Paint this picture in your mind in the most vivid way. It is important that you vividly feel yourself having what it is that you desire in your presence so that you can now touch, taste, smell, hear and see the things that would indicate that you are now in possession of your desires.

It is now time to make the sweetest most sensual love to this image. If you like, without replacing the images and senses of your desires, download the feeling of a phenomenal orgasm you might have had with a lover. Remember how amazing and satisfying it was. Now again, in your mind's eye, picture yourself with the things that you desire and the senses associated with having them. Breathe deeply and expansively, breathe in as if you feel yourself about to climax and breathe out again. Feel graphicly a sensation of deep satisfaction and gratitude departing from your essence. Again keep your desires of what you want to touch, taste, see, hear and smell in your imagination. Breathe in again deeply and orgasmically. Work your way up into a climax of deep satisfaction knowing that you have the things which you desire right here, right now. Finally, breathe out with a sense of deep satisfaction and gratitude. Repeat this prana breathing process for a moment or two, making the breaths deeper yet shorter, deeper and shorter, deeper and shorter. Shorter and faster, shorter and faster, shorter and faster until you reach a climax of gratitude and feel satisfied enough to let the orgasmic manifestation go. Breathe out slowly. Feel how amazing it feels in your heart to have been intimate with the things you desire the most. Be here for a moment. Let every cell of your being be filled with the light of the life force vitality.

Congratulations. You just impregnated the infinite sea of thoughts and desires, the primordial waters from which all things are born. The same waters that carried your wonderful self here to this realm of five senses via the drive of your father and the haven of your mother's womb all those years ago. Be gratified in knowing that this technique has worked and like any pregnancy, it takes time to grow. Don't keep touching your mind every five seconds to see if it worked or watch tarot card readers to see if they can predict when in time the manifestation will appear. A pregnant woman does not constantly go to the hospital to ask when the due date is, nor does she check the baby's heart every hour of the day. The impregnated woman knows she is pregnant and patiently waits the nine months that it takes to sufficiently grow a healthy baby and you must do the same. Don't pray on it or obsess over this technique. Yes, you can perform this technique more than once for your satisfaction, but do it only for your satisfaction, not for your obsession. Only the divine order of life knows how long it will take for perfect alignment across the entire cosmos to assemble so that you may meet your manifestation.

Remain patient and most importantly believe that it has been done unto you and that you will receive your manifestation and you will. Soon you will begin to see a flow of movement in the form of actions and interactions with others. This organic cohesion will move you in the direction of what it is that you want. You can also change the desires of the heart at any time, however, once this technique has been done, know that a powerful wave of attraction has been sent out and it must be transformed somewhere somehow. Use this technique for good and for the benefit of others to see speedy results. Never doubt whether this has worked or not. Doubt will surely set a strong wave in the opposite direction and smoulder the process. Imagine you are in bed with your lover about to tap out and you start thinking about how they possibly cheated on you with your best friend. What do you think is going to happen to that orgasm containing life force energy? Exactly, it's going to stop right there party over. So be sure to mind your thoughts. When you look back on what you just did here, it should be as satisfying as that memory you had earlier when you experienced the best orgasm of your life. Any frustration or ill-feeling towards what you just did here will hinder its performance.

How are you feeling? If you need to get a drink or some tissues perhaps, go ahead and do that. If you are ready for the rest of the show, however, let's hear a little story of a divine manifester who used the tantra technique very potently to manifest not one but two royal kingdoms which were not hers by birthright. Can you guess who's story I'm going to tell? That's right the goddess, Queen Cleopatra VII of Ptolemaic.

In 48 BC, the journey for this master of tantra manifestation was set into motion after the young Cleopatra was exiled from her throne by her younger siblings. Destined to a life of shame and even death if she were ever to enter her own country, the future for Cleopatra looked rather bleak. Cleopatra however believed herself to be from a lineage of gods and a reincarnation of the goddess Isis/Auset herself. She, therefore, did not claim such a shameful affliction onto her divine being. Instead, Cleopatra decided to harness the power of sexual allurement to cast a daring yet powerful spell on one of the greatest leaders in history.

One evening Julius Caesar, leader of Rome, had come to visit Egypt to ensure that the two empires had sound political relations despite all the challenges and changes facing Egypt's descending rulership. Cleopatra, having heard word of Caesar's visit, knew that this may be her only opportunity to put in a powerful play to attract what it was she desired the most. To rule an empire. That evening, while Caesar was in his court having a private meeting with his officials, a guardsman knocked on their door and interrupted their strategy meeting. He announced that a delivery had come for him and was waiting to be presented at his regal command. It was the dead of night and the announcement had taken the men off guard. Slightly bemused and highly curious, Caesar accepted the delivery to be made. The Guardsman left and soon returned with a rolled-up carpet which was adorned in beautiful tapestry and laced with attraction. As the guardsman presented the mysterious gift before Caesar and his men, he carefully rolled the carpet out before them only to reveal a sensually dressed queen Cleopatra, blossoming before them at the ripe age of just twenty-one.

Completely captivated by her enchantment, Caesar fell under Cleopatra's spell. That night, he protected her from her enemies by guarding her in the sanctuary of his bed. Their rendezvous was the beginning of one of the most famous yet fatal love affairs ever known. Cleopatra's love spell had the greatest leader of that dynasty completely devoted to her. He announced her as the legitimate ruler of Egypt and allied her in replacing her brother's reign. The debts Egypt owed to Rome were almost a thing of the past. Things were looking up for Cleopatra but her quest for global domination was not quite over yet. For some time Cleopatra continued to seduce Caesar with flamboyant displays of a nymph-like nature. Drowning in his desire for her, Caesar almost forgot about

his wife and life in Rome which was to the severe
disappointment of his officials and people across the
Mediterranean sea.

Soon enough, as is expected when one indulges in
lovemaking, Cleopatra fell pregnant. Caesar, unaware of her
pregnancy at the time, returned to Rome due to pressures
from his subjects and kinsmen. The seasons passed and
Cleopatra gave birth to a little boy who she named Ptolemy
Caesar or Caesarion for short. When Cleopatra visited Rome
in her usual splendour, she presented Caesar's illegitimate
child before his wife Calpurnia and his generals who all
witnessed the great leader claim the scandalous son. His acts
were seen as treacherous for he was subsequently announcing
Caesarion, his only son, as the heir to the Roman empire.
Cleopatra had manifested it all and primarily if not solely
through the energy of tantra.

After such a spectacle of adultery and liberalism, not only
against his wife but the Roman empire in itself, Caesar was
soon murdered by members of his court. Cleopatra was
forced to flee back to her throne in Egypt with her son
Ptolemy Caesar. Cleopatra would have to re-strategies how
she would conquer the Roman empire, seeing as the Roman
court would not accept a 'bastard' child as the heir of Caesar.

Queen Cleopatra, being a bit of a one-trick pony, invited
Mark Anthony, a powerful and influential war general of
Rome, to Egypt. While there she engulfed him in his deepest
pleasure: banquets, binge drinking and orgies. Mark Anthony,
drunk with satisfaction, fell under Queen Cleopatra's spell
and like Caesar became devoted to the realisation of her

desires. He spent his days in Egypt pampered with loot and lust. He even began to dress in the ways of the Egyptians, turning his back on the traditions of Rome. Mark Anthony however was a brute force warrior and eventually was called back to Rome by his duty to lead his army.

The official ruler of Rome, Octavian, who was Caesar's nephew, offered to Mark Anthony his sister's hand in marriage as a placebo for weaning Mark Anthony off of Cleopatra's seductive opioid. However, his duty as second in command along with the sensibilities of one of Rome's most beautiful bachelorettes was not enough to deafen the sound of the siren's call.

Just three years later, Mark Anthony returned to Egypt solely to serve Cleopatra as ruler of Rome and goddess over his heart. Mark Anthony attempted to legitimise Ptolemy Caesar as the legitimate ruler of Rome and Cleopatra as his legal wife; however, his efforts were met with resistance. The Roman empire had grown tired of Cleopatra's conquest to conquer their nation through seductive sorcery and so began a series of great battles to overthrow the intolerable power couple. After a heart-wrenching defeat on Greek waters, Anthony and Cleopatra both knew that the attraction had run its course and was now magnetising the karmic residue of greed, lust and power. Mark Anthony, as an honourable defeated soldier, fell on his sword. After realising she had lost a hand she could not recoup a third time, Cleopatra took her own life by inviting a poisonous snake to bite her breast so that she could ascend the earth as a true goddess. And so lives on the spirit of Cleopatra, free to reincarnate on earth as and when she pleases.

Caution to the reader. The use of tantra and sexual energy to manifest is no joke.

Cleopatra died of suicide. Which should be enough warning to all. Only use these manifestation techniques for the purpose of good. Using these techniques for power, greed, vanity and selfishness will only ever send a flow of dissatisfaction back your way. Think about how it feels when you use sexual energy on yourself for the pure purpose of a few moments of pleasure and the energy that is given off after you climax. Yeah yuck. So you can see how that feeling alone can create karmic dissatisfaction when the tantra technique is used for low vibrational and vain purposes.

Clearly, Cleopatra's techniques were advanced and worked for a time, but the problem she faced was the fact that she used other people to channel this energy. Both Caesar and Anthony had their own separate agendas, commitments and duties that conflicted with Cleopatra's. Even if it appeared that she had managed to convince them to come around to her position, the end result, for each of them, clearly showed where they both truly stood in their hearts. In addition, Cleopatra used the tantra technique to satisfy vain desires of being 'ruler' over not one but two empires! It's always best to use these techniques to lift the vibration of the entire collective consciousness. Use these techniques to see yourself celebrating with loved ones when they achieve what they have for so long strived for. Leave ego and selfishness behind and enjoy satisfying others while you satisfy yourself. This is the most powerful and righteous use of this technique. This leads us nicely along to our next chapter. How to manifest using the law of good.

4 THE POWER OF GOOD

First of all I would like to say, congratulations for making it this far. We live in a world where we are bombarded with distractions and it is seldom that we get a chance to do something that will improve ourselves. Self-care is paramount to our growth and the growth of the collective.

In this chapter, we are going to look at applying the law of good to bring forth the most powerful and prompt manifestation. When you decide to serve the divine intelligence in a way that brings about beneficial and desirable outcomes for the collective, you are using the power of good. The divine intelligence I speak of is the subtle force within all things that knows all, writes all and can bring forth all. Let's call this divine intelligence the All Consciousness. When you decide to work harmoniously with the All Consciousness, you are essentially placing yourself into the sea of collective thoughts that consists of all prayers, desires and non-desires ever known to man.

To demonstrate this, imagine that you live in an ocean without any bounds. The reason why this visualisation is so powerful is that you do live in an ocean; it is just less dense than the deep, salty fishy one we like to visit on our holidays. Every time someone has a thought, a small ripple is sent out and cascades throughout the ocean. This ripple at any time, and certainly at some point, will bump into someone as a small wave and cause them to be inspired by its effect on them. When someone's thought is intensified through sound aka speech, it makes a bigger wave. When someone's speech causes others to take immediate action, an even bigger wave ricochets throughout the ocean. When someone's thought causes many thousands or millions of people to act, a tsunami of influence is caused and that one initial thought possesses enough strength to completely change the landscape of collective living. With this in mind, if you have a thought that aims to hurt other beings, is controversial or is unprogressive to the collective consciousness, then it will be met with resistance when it bumps into the next person. This person will not feel the flow of inspiration to act in a way that reciprocates your intentions.

Let's say this differently as this is an abstract concept to understand. When you have a prayer, automatically the prayer is sent out to be answered. This prayer, however, can only be answered in a way that makes physical sense in relation to the collective thoughts and activities of everyone in the entire world. Unfortunately, you can not pray that everyone in the world gives you $10,000 and expect it to immediately happen because not everyone in the world has $10,000. Furthermore, not everyone in the world wants to freely give you $10,000 because of their reasons and ripples. If your prayer, however, included that you want everyone in the world to give you $10,000 in return that you may help to answer one of their prayers, then there is a good chance that a significant percentage of the world would find $10,000 so that their prayer would be answered.

The principle, outlined above, is using the laws of harmony and balance to bring forth heaven on earth. This principle is outlined clearly in the 42 laws of Maat. If you are unfamiliar with these 42 laws, you may be asking who on earth is Maat. Well, Maat isn't on earth at all. She is, in fact, an Egyptian deity known best for overseeing justice, balance and cosmic harmony. She is a goddess often depicted with a set of scales and expanded vulture wings. You have probably heard a folk tale or two about how when you die your heart is weighed against a feather. If your heart is heavier than a feather then you would not be accepted into heaven and will be condemned to an eternity of flames and fire. Either that or walk around the earth forevermore as an invisible ghost in purgatory. That lovely superstition comes directly from chapters 125-6 of The Egyptian Book Of The Dead. In this chapter, the deceased's heart is weighed against a feather on a set of scales before the great god Osiris. The deceased then declares a set of negative confessions, which is the 42 laws of Maat. These negative confessions are recited as followed.

1. I have not committed sin.
2. I have not committed robbery with violence.
3. I have not stolen.
4. I have not slain men or women.
5. I have not stolen food.
6. I have not swindled offerings.
7. I have not stolen from God/Goddess.
8. I have not told lies.
9. I have not carried away food.
10. I have not cursed.
11. I have not closed my ears to truth.
12. I have not committed adultery.
13. I have not made anyone cry.
14. I have not felt sorrow without reason.
15. I have not assaulted anyone.
16. I am not deceitful.
17. I have not stolen anyone's land.
18. I have not been an eavesdropper.
19. I have not falsely accused anyone.
20. I have not been angry without reason.
21. I have not seduced anyone's wife.
22. I have not polluted myself.
23. I have not terrorized anyone.
24. I have not disobeyed the Law.
25. I have not been exclusively angry.
26. I have not cursed God/Goddess.
27. I have not behaved with violence.
28. I have not caused disruption of peace.

29. I have not acted hastily or without thought.

30. I have not overstepped my boundaries of concern.

31. I have not exaggerated my words when speaking.

32. I have not worked evil.

33. I have not used evil thoughts, words or deeds.

34. I have not polluted the water.

35. I have not spoken angrily or arrogantly.

36. I have not cursed anyone in thought, word or deeds.

37. I have not placed myself on a pedestal.

38. I have not stolen what belongs to God/Goddess.

39. I have not stolen from or disrespected the deceased.

40. I have not taken food from a child.

41. I have not acted with insolence.

42. I have not destroyed property belonging to God/Goddess.

The 42 laws are ancient principles that rule over cosmic order and allow prayers and desires within the sea of thoughts to remain in harmony. Prayers which align with these 42 principles have a better chance of being answered. You may have recognised some of these principles as universal values of morality such as the 10 commandments. Some may even resonate as words of wisdom that your grandma tried to impress upon you while you were young. There is a reason why these principles are repeated and shared throughout history and why they have withstood the test of ancestral inheritance. That reason is that they allow an individual to go throughout the day enforcing the law of good. The 42 principles of Maat are a fantastic way to divinely define what the law of good is. The symbolic images that are drawn in the

Egyptian Book Of The Dead, were illustrated to remind you to keep your heart light and free of malice.

One who has a light heart, filled with good, can easily align themselves with the same forces of supreme beings who are powered by unconditional love. Unconditional love is the most powerful force that we as humans can comprehend here in this time. It is however not something that we often practice. Even if you go to some religious buildings, you may hear the pastor preaching about how unconditional love is only possible for God. You may also have heard the false narrative that all humans are sinners and therefore it is in vain to try and love in the way of a God. If you take anything from this book please make it this. Those teachings are untrue. If you have the power to love your mother, your children, your spouse or your friends, then you have the power to love unconditionally, just as God does. If you can wish good for other people, then you can carry a heart which is as light as a feather.

This ability to love from the heart is a supreme power that can be likened to that of a god. Granted, it is not always easy to love openly from the heart and the type of love spoken of here goes deeper than simply giving to your friend's go-fund-me page. Gods and goddesses understood very well that there is a sea of collective desires, rippling throughout the universe. These thoughts operate on principles such as correspondence meaning that chaotic and uncooperative thoughts can only give birth to chaotic and uncooperative situations. They also understood that the universe itself came into existence through the principle of unconditional love, therefore everything ever created is born out of love. If everything is born out of love, does it not make sense that you should use love to give birth to your manifestations? This is a rhetorical question, the answer is yes of course! So what kind of thoughts should you be having if you want to manifest a dream lifestyle? A mind that is using the power of good and a heart operating on unconditional love wants to see the collective society expand into greatness, progression and abundance. If you can observe greatness and abundance in others without judgement or jealousy, you open yourself up to receive the same kind of greatness and abundance. If you are constantly judging other people for enjoying their lives and expressing their abundance, then you are not in alignment with the law of good. In actuality, you are putting yourself in a current which is moving you further away from having these things yourself because you are viewing yourself as not having them.

Of course, it is human nature for us to see others with things and desire them. This is natural as we all desire to feel as though we are growing and expanding but it is not an excuse to be bitter and judgmental. It is much more beneficial to lighten your heart and rejoice when you see humanity manifesting their dreams as this is confirmation that you are also doing the same. This is the essence of the law of good and by wishing others well on their journeys, you are operating in the power of it.

Make it a habit to smile frequently and feel excited when you see others enjoying themselves and manifesting their desires. If it does not feel natural for you to do this, start forcing yourself to do it. Train yourself to be happy for others, even if it means forcing a toothy smile. Your brain can not tell the difference as to who, why and how it is smiling. Its programming is not as sophisticated as the mind. All it knows is that you have seen something that you desire and you are now smiling, indicating that you are happy. By-products of happiness, such as smiling, releases dopamine which is the reward neurotransmitter. Once dopamine is released, your brain will feed into your mind's activities so that you perform actions that will make you feel that emotion again. So even if you see the thing you desire to manifest on someone else, smile and rejoice in the observation that it is possible to manifest it. By expressing love and joy when seeing the thing you desire on someone else, you are creating a flow of love energy that will soon come back onto you. This is using the law of good. It's very subtle and simple but requires a tuning of the heart and mind to come into alignment with the heart and mind of God.

God operates on the frequency of unconditional love and to manifest like a god, you must too. For some, this will come very easily, especially if you are empathic and child-like in nature. However, I would say for 90% of the adult population, it is going to be a little bit more difficult as the current way of life often adulterates the hearts of man and causes them to turn cold. It is therefore your duty to begin to polish your heart and mind. Remove the soot and allow it to be free of ill will and selfishness. You can begin the renewing of your heart using this technique.

This technique is going to resemble something of a prayer. Whether you believe in a specific god or not you can still use this technique. If you believe in a god then for the purpose of this technique you can hold them as the subject for the prayer. If you do not believe in a god, then you can accept

that there is a supreme power that holds everything together
and keeps everything in harmony.

There is a single source of creation that knows everything
that has ever been and ever will be. You can think of this
source as being like the deep mysteries lying at the depths of
the primordial oceans. Its expansiveness is incomprehensible
such as that of outer space. Whatever you believe it doesn't
matter too much. The thing that matters the most when
using this technique is that you recognise there is a power
greater than you and that you are open to surrendering to it.
This is how we will begin our prayer.

Surrender completely to the supreme power or your god.
When you are surrendering, it is important that you feel
yourself submitting your perceived control over to the
infinite power. Allow your shoulders to drop and your jaw to
unclench. Take a deep breath, slow your breathing down and
just relax. Just melt into the hands of the one who is never
changing and forever. Allow all the responsibility for the
achievement of your desires to be in the hands of the power
which is of harmony and pure love. It is better to do this
prayer while alone and without disruption, although it can be
done anywhere.

Once you have successfully surrendered, next you will need
to connect to the collective consciousness of all. Earlier I
described this collective consciousness as the sea of thoughts.
For this technique, you can imagine yourself as being
underwater, silently witnessing all the prayers, thoughts and
ripples caused by others, gently happening around you. You
can also just be very still in this moment and connect to the
consciousness of the scene around you. You can listen to the

song of the birds outside, or feel the subtle kiss of the wind moving through your space. You may even choose to witness the tranquil rising and falling of your chest as you breathe in and out automatically. Observing your breath flowing in and out is a great way to get connected to the collective consciousness because the happening of your breath going in and out is the result of the All Consciousness. It is a surrendering operation as you, the person you know yourself to be, is not responsible for the automation of breathing yet you can connect to the phenomena by observing that it is taking place in you. It is the subconscious you who is responsible for its happening and it is through the subconscious that you connect to the All Consciousness.

Once you are connected, begin praying for others. You can do this out loud or in your head but you should unselfishly wish well for others you may know and also for the collective. Doing this while in a state of surrender and connection is highly effective as you are extremely close to the power of unconditional love. Allow this energy to flow through you freely. Raise your head and your palms to the sky and begin wishing well for others. Wish humanity peace and love. Offer your neighbour abundance and health. Pray for those who need healing and holding. Ask for them to be embraced by the unconditional love of the great I am and feel comforted by its embrace. Pray for the one who has been striving for their desires and is about to give up. Pray that they soon receive a breakthrough. Pray that the unhopeful will know a power as great as the one who operates on pure love and that the love might enter their hearts and guide them to a place of faith and belief.

Whatever your prayer is, just be sure that the overall theme gives light to another. When giving light to others, the ripples of good desires flow through the sea of thoughts and crashes into your consciousness dripping in unconditional love.

Once you have prayed, keep the palms of your hands raised to the sky. Ask the one you have surrendered to, to fill your hands up with the thing you desire the most. Imagine your hands overflowing with your desires. Try to feel the sensation of receiving in your hands. Feel them getting heavier and use your imagination to envision yourself holding the things which you desire. Make sure that this time you are asking for yourself. Asking for yourself is important because you can do more good for others when you have the tools, freedom and happiness to be the best you. Ask for your wildest dreams to come to you in significant abundance however, do not ask from a place of desperation. Always ask to receive from a place of surrender and unconditional love. You will know you have done this correctly when you can ask for your desires without feeling attached to the outcome. By having undeniable faith that the All Consciousness is working on your manifestation, you can channel its ultimate power.

Once you have finished asking, put your palms together and feel yourself in possession of all that you have asked for. Concentrate on your heart and express gratitude for having received the things which you now have in your hands. Smile, laugh or cry if you feel to. An emotional reaction wrapped in gratitude will magnetise the flow of desire, moving a stronger current towards you. By expressing gratitude in a place of surrender, connectedness and goodwill, you are accepting that you have received your desires and that they are on their way to you. How and when your desires will come to you are out of your control however you accept that you have given your control over to the same force that keeps your heart beating 24/7. Stay in this moment of prayer and observation for as long as it feels natural to you. When you are ready to go on with the rest of your day, be at peace and feel deep satisfaction that all you desire for yourself and others are swimming through the sea of thoughts, making their way to the shore of your physical existence.

If anyone knew about using the law of good to manifest a life of peace, love and riches it was the infamous King Solomon. Whenever the phrase blessed and highly favoured is mentioned, King Solomon automatically comes to mind for his life was nothing short of justice and plentitude. In 1010 B.C, King Solomon was born the tenth son of King David and his mother was Bathsheba, the widow of his brother Uriah. Although he was not the first son of David and therefore traditionally not the first in line for the throne, King David had been loyal and dedicated to God in all his years of reign and God saw it fit that Solomon would continue David's reign over Israel. It was said to David that Solomon would proceed with David's success and give glory to the kingdom of God and Israel in his honour. When David was in his last moments, Bathsheba went to his side over concerns she had witnessed in the royal court. She told David that his firstborn son, Adonijah, had been parading around the palace acting as if he was already king. It was clear from his relationships and activities with court officials, that Adonijah was making plans to acquire the throne after David had passed. Adonijah was assuming himself, king, even though he knew that Solomon had been promised the throne. To Solomon and Bathebath this was treasonous against God, which Bathebath made known to David. David agreed that Solomon was promised as his successor and so he held a crowning ceremony for him to make it certified. On the day of his accession, Zodak, who was the high priest and Nathan the esteemed prophet, anointed Solomon as the official King for all to see. He took his place on his father's throne and became the King of Israel. His people's rejoicing roared throughout the city and met the ear of Adonijah. Adonijah became fearful as he knew that what he had attempted to do was treacherous. Fearing for his life, Adonijah went to the holy place to repent and ask for forgiveness. Solomon, at the grand old age of 15, observed Adonijah's repenting and told him that he was forgiven so long as he behaved himself. The day came when David was to say his goodbyes, as he prepared to return to the home of god. On his deathbed, he pulled Solomon close and told him of these things:

"I am about to go the way of all the earth, so bestrong, act like a man, and observe what the Lord your God requires: Walk in obedience to him, and keep his decrees and commands, his laws and regulations, as written in the Law of Moses. Do this so that you may prosper in all you do and wherever you go and that the Lord may keep his promise to me: 'If your descendants watch how they live, and if they walk faithfully before me with all their heart and soul, you will never fail to have a successor on the throne of Israel.'"

Solomon, although young, accepted his father's decree with a righteous heart. David passed peacefully of natural causes and Solomon took reign of the throne without objections. With such a heavy crown to carry and big boots to fill, young Solomon took his heart to God and said to him these things:

"Now, Lord my God, you have made your servant king in place of my father David. But I am only a little child and do not know how to carry out my duties. Your servant is here among the people you have chosen, a great people, too numerous to count or number. So give your servant a discerning heart to govern your people and to distinguish between right and wrong. For who is able to govern this great people of yours?"

The Lord was pleased that Solomon had asked for this. So God said to him,

"Since you have asked for this and not for long life or wealth for yourself, nor have asked for the death of your enemies but for discernment in administering justice, I will do what you have asked. I will give you a wise and discerning heart, so that there will never have been anyone like you, nor will there ever be. Moreover, I will give you what you have not asked for—both wealth and honour—so that in your lifetime you will have no equal among kings. And if you walk in obedience to me and keep my decrees and commands as David your father did, I will give you a long life."

Then Solomon awoke—and he realized it had been a dream.
- Kings

Solomon's promise to God was quickly tested when he had to make some brutally tough decisions to firmly secure his position as King. Adonijah was sitting alone in his quarters feeling bitter and unjustly done by. It was tradition for the firstborn to be named successor of the throne and after having a taste for power, posing as king in the last days of his father, Adonijah's ambitions to reign lingered within him. That evening Adonijah called Bathsheba, Solomon's mother, to his quarters in secrecy. He pleaded with his stepmother to persuade Solomon to allow him to marry the late King David's dearly favoured concubine. Knowing that Solomon was young and impressionable, Adonijah believed that feeding the request through his beloved mother would conceal his intentions to legitimise himself on the throne of David. When Bathsheba went to Solomon with Adonijah's request, he transparently saw through his cunning half-brother's plots, as if looking into clear spring water at his own reflection. Solomon called upon the wisdom blessed unto him and ordered for his brother to be killed. Solomon had to make several bloody and difficult decisions but did so all in the name of righteousness and by the wisdom of the discerning heart that he had asked God for.

For forty years of royal reign, Solomon lived in a way of divine righteousness and adorned the nation of Israel with a fortune of good, peace and prosperity. Every year Solomon would graciously receive in excess of six hundred and sixty-six talents of gold which is around twenty-one thousand kilos or twenty-two tonnes! King Solomon, lavish in his manifestations, materialised a great throne made of ivory which was regally embellished in gold. It had six lions on either side and a court of loyal subjects surrounding it. The lands he governed overflowed with grain and cattle. The ships he voyaged, valiantly returned with decks filled with gold, silver, jewels and spices. King Solomon had great treaties with pharaohs, generals and royals from lands afar. All who came in his presence gifted him with splendour and were honoured to be in his presence, including the queen of Sheba. The queen had heard rumours of his divinity and as she was a wise and spiritual woman herself, wanted to see if all the rumours about Solomon were true or merely an exaggeration. Upon her visit to Solomon's seat, queen Sheeba spoke these words:

"The report I heard in my own country about your achievements and your wisdom is true. But I did not believe these things until I came and saw with my own eyes. Indeed, not even half was told me; in wisdom and wealth you have far exceeded the report I heard. How happy your people must be! How happy your officials, who continually stand before you and hear your wisdom! Praise be to the Lord your God, who has delighted in you and placed you on the throne of Israel. Because of the Lord's eternal love for Israel, he has made you king to maintain justice and righteousness."

The good that Solomon bestowed onto Israel was paid back to Solomon tenfold. With seven hundred wives and three hundred concubines, Solomon's bloodline has permeated the DNA of humanity. There are even many individuals in society today who can still trace their lineage directly back to him, including Haile Selassie I.

Spectacular right? Although many of the accounts for Solomon come in the form of religious text, do not be put off if you do not consider yourself religious or of the same religion as King Solomon. The whole point of this lesson is to understand how using the law of good and righteousness always creates great gifts in return. King Solomon purified his heart from a young age and genuinely wanted to do good for all the people of Israel in the name and love of his father David. King Solomon frequently gave offerings to his God, the All Consciousness, who is pumping your heart right now without you even thinking about it.

King Solomon loved to do right by his people. He treated his servants with dignity and offered fair wages to those who worked for him. He gave leaders a place to lead and was just in his judgements (if you don't know about King Solomon's famous judgement I advise you to go look it up, just so you can see how wise this man is). The reason why King Solomon was held in such glory still to this day was that he embodied the principle of using the law for good. This point is significantly illustrated when the Law of Moses was mentioned when King David gave Solomon his blessing. These laws include the 10 commandments, which can be directly associated with the 42 laws of Maat. David knew by giving his son Solomon these instructions to follow, that he could not fail to live a prosperous life. For this reason, the great I am, the invisible force, God, the creator, the universe, whatever you want to call it, favoured him greatly and made him an example of what the power of good can do for an individual.

5 Thoughts

In the chapter on meditation we left off on the lifelong teachings of Buddha which can be found in the Dhammapada. These teachings withstand the test of time and reflect many of the teachings known in the modern and ancient world. The fundamental takehome of these teaching is this: You become what you think about. Each day that goes by, you create who you are and what you are through the majority of thoughts you have about yourself. Earl Nightingale kindly puts this in another way through his famous quote:

"A man or a woman becomes what they think about all day long."

One thing that makes humans unique from other sentient creatures on this earth is our ability to think. It is also the thing that limits our abilities and turns us into fools when not used correctly. The fact of the matter is that people take their minds for granted because it was given to them for free. The majority of us are unaware of the powerful tool that exists inside of our heads. The mind is a transformative and manifesting machine that performs its mechanics with every thought that you have, good or bad.

To think that God is a big bearded man that lives in the sky, deciding your fate is to give your power away to an illusion. God is your own colourful human imagination. Whatever you think of, whatever images you are crafting in your mind, manifests into this physical realm. The power of God exists within your imagination. Whenever you have a thought, you are communicating with the God force, the All Consciousness, and asking for it to create whatever it is that you are imagining. If you like, you can visualise a little genie living inside of your mind. Everything you say to yourself, the genie hears and grants every wish that your imagination makes.

You're probably thinking if there is a genie inside of my mind granting me my wishes then why am I not the richest person in the world yet? Or why haven't I found the love of my life? Well, the truthful answer to this is, that you have not yet mastered your mind. Although you may have thoughts about obtaining material things or living with the person you love the most, every so often you likely also have a flood of thoughts that are counter progressive to those of your deepest desires. For example, you may have thoughts about being the richest person in the world in one thought but then in a second thought, you may have thoughts about not being able to pay off your debts. Both of these thoughts are created in imagination and the magical genie hears and grants them all. These two opposing thoughts are conflicting and therefore create resistance to achieving one's most burning desires. To be able to manifest at a more consistent and deterministic rate, you must become a master of your mind. You must consistently produce thoughts that relate most significantly to who it is that you wish to be rather than who you currently believe yourself to be.

To become the master of your mind is the most laborious and lengthy task that a man or woman will have the pleasure of taking on in their lifetime. This is because the mind is a stubborn mule and inherently ignorant of the power which lies within it. It is fickle and almost as elusive as the wind. It is egotistical and judgemental of self and others. It is comfortable to re-run all the old programming stored in the subconscious from early childhood, programs which no longer serve you, and too lazy to turn on anything else. The mind can be your best friend or your fatal enemy. You must begin to cultivate your mind in a way that is harmonious with your wants and needs, just as soon as you latch onto this understanding. But before we begin to train the mind to be a cooperating component in our life, let's first understand the various types of thoughts one can have and what the implications for having them are:

Fear doubt and indecision

Unfortunately we find that the majority of people we meet nowadays are operating in the thought patterns of fear, doubt and indecision. At the time of writing, the UK is experiencing a 'petrol shortage'. The shortage comes not because the UK has run out of petrol, but because the vast majority of people are living with thoughts of fear, doubt and indecision. These thoughts of fear have crystalised into the action of 'panic buying' and they have therefore self-prophesied the fuel shortage. These people are now put into a position of slavish dependency on the government and expect the organisation to 'bail' them out of this fuel shortage situation. They depend on the resolution of others, even though it was their own fear that put them in the situation.

Fearful thoughts also go hand in hand with indecision. Many people are too afraid to think for themselves. They simply do not want to have the responsibility for making important decisions for themselves and would prefer someone else, like the government, to make those decisions for them. Again if a man (or a woman) cannot make a decision for themselves, they begin to practice weak and sheepish habits. This type of person just goes along with the crowd and allows others to drive the powerful machine responsible for the direction their life takes. Many of these people find themselves dependent on a system that has failed them over and over again, but their inability to think and make decisions for themselves makes them slavishly dependent on these systems.

Doubt, finally, is another weak thought that stops a man from being able to obtain his true desires. You may practice all the meditation, tantra and yoga techniques in the world, but if doubt begins to harvest in the mind, one will begin to partake in habits that are irregular and fretful. An opportunity which would bring you closer to your desires may pop up on your doorstep but because of doubts such as believing nothing good can happen, you may miss the opportunity. Don't be stuck in the thoughts of 'it's too good to be true'. Many of the greatest opportunities came to successful people because they took the risk on something 'too good to be true'. The too good to be true opportunities can be the big break that is needed, so do away with fear and step out of your comfort zone.

Laziness and apathetic thoughts.

Laziness and a nonchalant attitude are thought processes that also limit a man's ability to manifest his desires. You often find these people indifferent to any position. They might indulge in smoking weed or having a glass or two in front of the telly every evening. These habits practised over a long time manifest disorder and uncleanliness in one's life. A person with lazy thoughts is a dreamer. It is the person who has one thousand things that they are going to do but when you ask them what actions they are taking to achieve this, they reply: "well that's in the future". You may hear them come up with yet another excuse which prevents them from actually having to take any action in the present moment.

Apathetic thoughts go hand in hand with lazy thoughts. Apathetic thoughts are like going to bed with the supermodel of your dreams and finding yourself unable to perform. Your passions and desires want you just as much as you are wanting them but with apathetic thoughts, thoughts that lack the proper interest, one becomes indifferent to the outcome.

These thoughts practised over a long period create a bad attitude of non-belief in the forthcoming reality. These habits eventually crystallize into situations which are filled with confusion and laziness. A person may display an attitude of entitlement to the things they want, even though they barely even get hard for them. They may say things like the rich are lucky and who cares about possessing desires, we will all die one day anyway. Although this is true, we will all die, we are also currently living and therefore it should be in our greatest interest to live a life we can be proud of.

Laziness in thought also leads to dishonest behaviour or beggary. Some may try to skip corners to manifest what they want by tricking others or by pulling on the emotions of their peers to plead for charity. Although the desired things may come to the individual, they may not last long in their existence because the thought processes used to obtain them are limiting and a consequence of 'luck'.

Resentful condemnation

People whose thoughts are possessed with resentfulness and condemnation will surely begin to practice judgemental and violent habits. This is not to say that if you have resentful feelings you will become a gang banger but perhaps your behaviour will be passive-aggressive. You may find yourself giving people evil looks for no particular reason or enjoy cutting people off on the motorway just because you felt valid in doing so. Over time, this judgmental and passive-aggressive behaviour will crystallise into situations of violence and persecution. Maybe someone will eventually come out of their car and demand a fistfight because you almost crashed into their car trying to overtake them in traffic. Maybe your application for a job will not be accepted because the interviewer recognises you from five years ago when you gave her the resentful glare of death while she was taking too long in the queue at the supermarket.

Whatever the circumstances, having thoughts which judge others, will only cause an individual to behave in a way which pushes people away and attracts confrontation and unnecessary anger. If this is you, drop your shoulders and wish good to people you see, whether you know them or not. Sending love and acceptance in the way of others automatically attracts love and acceptance into your own life.

Beauty

In contrast, beautiful thoughts of every kind lead you to practice behaviours which are graceful and tender. These types of thoughts colour the world around you and you will begin to see as the angels do. If you begin to think about how amazing it is to be here now because everything is made of unconditional love, if you believe that everyone is just trying the best that they can, your world will brighten up before you. If you can recognise that like screaming, raging toddlers most people just need a hug, your days will be full of sunshine and individuals who want to help and support you will magnetically be attracted to your energy.

Beautiful thoughts are like midnight moonbeams. They often go unseen but they are the driving force that makes the seed germinate. Beautiful thoughts are the unexplainable energy creating the supportive wave which gives the surfer a surface to ride on. If you are someone who has for most of their life practised pessimistic, low vibrational thoughts then you won't be instantly gratified by saying something nice about someone in your head. It takes practice. First, you will have to begin to catch yourself when you are in a negative, nasty thought stream and then lighten these thoughts up by transmuting them into more neutral pleasant thoughts. Over time you will begin to exercise more neutral and loving thoughts. When you catch yourself having nasty thoughts you will begin to ask yourself, "why would I say something like that? That's not me." The habit of beautiful thoughts will begin to crystallize into situations which reflect your grace and tenderness. Your heavenly aura will shine out from your very being and others will not be able to resist your angelic glow.

Selflessness

When an individual can sit at the centre of the world, free of all attachments and expectations, they adopt a greater sense of awareness. After consistent observation, this individual will come to realise that everything they watch is only a detached aspect of themselves; like rays of light emitted from their own sun. Consider this thought for a moment. If everything that you observe is simply a reflection of yourself, good or bad, would it not be in your interest to treat all things with respect and goodwill? One who possesses selflessness has a sense that their existence is of best use when it is in service to others because being in service to others, is being of service to oneself.

Someone who has thoughts to be a helpful individual and of service to others will create tangible habits of self-control and temperance. He is the calm husband who does not raise his hand to his wife when she is highly emotional. She is the nurturing mother who lends her body to her infant, for a time, so that they may be nurtured and comforted by her motherly embrace. If you are selfless you have self-control and discipline and as a result, much peace and resolve will be attracted to you. We all speak of how we want peace right? Well, begin with your thoughts. Instead of arguing with a heated individual, think selfless thoughts and think "how can I be of service to this distressed person." Sometimes that can be as simple as restraining oneself from reacting and walking out the room selflessly, without the need to defend the ego. It could be to share your talents or activism so that you can raise the collective consciousness or can make someone's life a little easier. Whatever the resolve, someone who embodies selfless thoughts begin to practice principles of unconditional love and therefore bliss and harmony will be a constant in their life.

Courage

A wise man once said that in today's society, the opposite of courage is not cowardness, it's conformity. A courageous person believes in themselves. Courageous thoughts consist of positive affirmations and meaningful mantras which lift the spirit of the individual. These courageous, encouraging thoughts lead an individual to form habits which foster self-reliance and decisions which relate to the true will of the individual. These types of thoughts can be as simple as saying to yourself: "I can do this, this does work, I am going to do this, nothing can stop me from having this, I am not afraid to fall because I will get back up again". This type of positive self-talk manifests strength in you.

Those who can valiantly speak to themselves positively, despite what is happening around them, possess the resilience to overcome any situation. Because of the strength within them, the individual will live a life of great freedom as they do not have to rely on anything outside of themselves for fear of failure. These individuals will see what they wish to see and have what they want to have because they have the strength from courageous thoughts, to relentlessly go after what they want in life. If you can take anything from these words, take this; in a world of conforming cowards, dare to speak life into yourself. Know it is perfectly okay to be yourself and in truth, it is extremely brave to hold onto your morals and ideals even in the face of condemnation. Continue to believe in yourself by observing the words you say and just watch how the strength to do what you feel comes to you while freedom embraces you.

Energetic

Energetic thoughts are the ones that spur you into action. These thoughts are the ones where the individual imagines themselves at the peak of the mountain they wish to climb. They see themselves covered in gold medals with a press team flashing cameras in awe of the achievement. Energetic thoughts are the ones that tell you to push through the pain when performing a workout so that you can complete a few extra sets. Energetic thoughts materialize into habits of industriousness, which in turn crystallizes into situations of achievement and ideal manifestation. Energetic thoughts make the individual get up and go after everything they want without any doubts about its obtainment.

Energetic thoughts are masculine and encouraging in nature. In the mind, these thoughts sound like: "let's go, this is easy, go a little harder, push yourself further, keep going, we are going to celebrate hard once this is achieved". It is these thoughts that keep you from laziness and motivate you into action. Action is vital for the process of any manifestation, things can not appear unless the right energy and effort are put behind them.

Kind and loving

The individual whose mind is nourished with kind and loving thoughts can never be short of kindness and love. A person who has kindness and love in their mind becomes a person with considerate actions. Kind thoughts crystallize into behaviours such as letting someone in a shopping queue go ahead of you because they only have a few items. Kind thoughts grow from considering how it would make someone's day to pay them a compliment or to visit an old relative who you haven't seen in a while. Kind and loving thoughts are naturally seeking situations that give birth to gratitude. Whenever these thoughts are practised, they materialise circumstances where 'Thank you" will be vocalised.

A person who is innately considerate of others is a person who will create situations of abiding comfort. It takes just a few moments to consider another person's well-being. Just a simple action as holding the door open for someone who has a lot of shopping, or giving a crying child a lollipop, creates a great gift of gratitude to be shared among comrades. When you create a moment of considerate action, you have been of service to someone else and that someone else has expressed and felt gratitude. This state of gratitude sends a karmic wave of feelings of thankfulness back to you. In this sense, karma simply means cause and effect, which we will go into more detail about in a later chapter. The law of cause and effect means that the kindness shown by you will be expressed back in kindness and gifts from the universe, which makes life a more blissful experience.

Somewhere in 1600 BC lived a man named Job. Residing with his wife and ten children, Job was an honourable man who had accumulated a grandeur of wealth. His money and business were so amplified by the abundance that he had a great number of employees across the land of Uz. Despite his monopoly of wealth, Job remained faithful and fearful of the Lord and sought to be upright in all his ways. Externally, Job was blameless however Job would often become possessed with perverted thoughts about his children's activities. Because of his obsession with righteousness and fear that his children had sinned, Job would prepare burnt offerings after each celebration his children would have so that they could be purified. For many years, Job was blessed by the grace of God however one day he came to his judgement.

The sons of the Lord who governed earth yet resided in heaven, came together to assess Job and his seemingly sinless ways. It was true that Job's thoughts of righteousness had for many years won favour with the Lord who had blessed him with bountiful abundance. Despite this Satan, who was also a son of the Lord, considered Job and deemed that if it was not for all his outward possessions which made his life easy, he would cease to be a righteous man and would begin to have thoughts that persecute God. Satan's judgement was accepted and the Lord gave Satan instruction to do what he willed on the achievements of Job.

Back on earth, it was Job's eldest son's birthday and his other seven sons and three daughters were celebrating in his quarters. As they were celebrating, one of Job's servants came running frantically to Job's tent. The servant who came before Job was tainted with terror as he bared bad news onto Job. The servant told Job that thieves of a foreign land had come and attacked all of the workmen who were tending to Job's oxen and donkeys. In their struggle, the thieves slaughtered all the attendants and made off with the animals. The servant was the sole survivor of the attack.

The servant had barely finished delivering the bad news when another of Job's helpers came charging into the tent. Barely able to catch his breath, the horrified helper told job that a forest fire had broken out where his sheep were grazing and that fire had devoured all of his sheep. The messenger told Job that his shepherds had tried to save the livestock but in their attempts, they too were devoured by the flames and he was the only survivor.

Just then another one of Job's workmen came bellowing in to tell Job that a raiding party had murdered his workmen who were guarding his camels and had made off with the animals. The workman was the sole survivor, fated to deliver Job the misfortune. Before Job could even process the information, one more messenger came to Job and told him that a mighty wind had blown in from the desert, dismantling all four corners of his eldest son's house where his children were feasting. The house had collapsed onto Job's offspring, killing them all. Job rose from where he was seated and stripped himself bare. He shaved his head and threw himself on the cold ground, naked and blameless as the day he was born. He proceeded to worship the Lord, proclaiming that it was the Lord who had given Job his achievements and now it was also the Lord who had taken it all away. Even in utter devastation, Job remained faithful to his God and upright in his thoughts.

Once again the sons of the Lord came to meet with the supreme one who resides in heaven. The Lord of lords turned to Satan in observation of Job and told him that, despite allowing Satan to ruin him, Job remained a righteous and god-fearing man. Satan displeased that his reasoning had been doubted, theorised that Job was willing to give up his material possessions so that he would experience a blissful afterlife however if Job was to give up his body, he would not remain so honourable. The Lord, intrigued by Satan's reasoning, permitted Satan to strike down on Job's flesh with the condition that he was not to kill him.

With that, Satan entered the place where Job was resting and bombarded his body with blistering boils. Job's flesh began to betray him however he still praised the Lord. Job sat in the ashes of his dead skin as it peeled away from his body by the fire. His wife watched him in dismay and asked him why he remained faithful to the Lord when the Lord had given him a body that resembled the deceased to live in. Surely if cursed the Lord and don away with him, his body would depart from Job's spirit and he could finally be at peace. Job, somewhat outraged at what his wife had said to him, called her foolish and said that it was just as right to praise the Lord for the hard times as it was to praise him for the good times. And so Job remained faithful to the Lord and upright in his thoughts.

Word spread of Job's suffering and soon after his three friends: Eliphaz, Bildad and Zophar travelled from afar to visit him. When they saw his almost unrecognisable state, they wept for his agony and sat with him in silence for seven days and seven nights. The silence was finally broken by Job whose pain had reached its peak and the suffering from his body had finally reached his mind. When he spoke he cursed the day he was born saying these words:

"May the day of my birth perish…may God above not care about it; may no light shine upon it…may blackness overwhelm it…may no shout of joy be heard in it…may it wait for daylight in vain…why did I not perish at birth…I would be asleep and at rest with the kings who ruled the earth…why is light given to those in misery…to those who

long for death which does not come…What I feared has come upon me…I have no peace…only turmoil."

Job cursed his life and wished for death and it was the first time anyone had ever heard him speak this way. Disturbed by Job's narration, Eliphaz spoke out against what Job had attested to. Eliphaz reminded Job of the righteous life he had lived and declared that surely because Job had lived such a good life, God would find favour in him and restore his life to one of abundance and prosperity. Eliphaz reminded Job to remain faithful to God even though he was troubled by him. Eliphaz gave this advice to his frail friend because he believed that only God has the power to vindicate Job from his suffering. Job did not take too kindly to what Eliphaz had to say for his suffering was like the winter sun on the horizon; blinding him from all hope and faith in anything. With the words which followed, Job rejected Eliphaz's solace and also God's perceived mercy in the process.

Bildad interjected Job's cries and once again reminded Job that although he was suffering the fate of the godless, Job had been an upright man all his life and did not deserve to go through the predicament that he found himself in. Bildad suggested that he make a case to God and plea for his mercy, for if he was truly a righteous man, then God would end his suffering. Once again Job scoffed at the advice of his friend. Although he believed himself to be righteous, he now doubted the justness of God. Job especially doubted that such an omnipotent power would have any time or concern for his mere mortal life and could not see how praying would do him any good. Job had seemingly lost all faith and wished for death more than anything.

The last of Job's friends, Zophar, having listened to all that had been said, spoke out against them. Zophar expressed that somewhere in his timeline Job must have sinned, for God was just and only brought terror onto evildoers. Zophar told Job to find a reason as to why God would do this wicked thing to him and to repent, for it would be the only way for him to end his suffering. Zophar's words were the last straw for Job. He announced to his friends that their wisdom was of no use to him. He had spent many years on earth as a healthy and experienced man. He had spent many days in the presence of God and had had many prayers answered. He knew the ways of God of which his friends had argued to aid him however, there was a way of God, a wisdom of the deep, that he did not know and clearly neither did his friends. Job then agreed that he should go before God, not to repent for sins or beg for mercy or anything of that kind, but to attain the greater mysteries of the omnipotent power.

Job stood in his self-righteousness yet his friends disagreed with what he had to say. Each friend, one by one condemned Job and gave arguments as to why all these things were happening to him. Their arguments claimed that somewhere within Job's ways, wickedness dwelled for god only punishes those who have wicked ways. Job, utterly unimpressed by his so-called friends' condemnation of his character, argued that many wicked men live seemingly wonderful lives despite all the trouble they bring to the earth. Even though his friends had a lot to say about the nature of God, Job refused to accept that he was at fault for the hardships that had come to him. Job strongly believed that only God had a power great enough to bring such adversity onto him. God was the one who suspended the earth in the sky and the one who divided the skies from the sea by drawing out the horizon. Job could not believe that righteousness had anything to do with God's reasoning for his anguish. There had to be another layer of wisdom, not common to the common man, a pearl of wisdom that would explain all that had happened to Job.

And just like that, for a brief moment, Job's mind was flooded with thoughts from the days where grace adorned his shoulders and gratitude to God was the theme of his days. He began to speak of beautiful times when: *"God's intimate friendship blessed my house...my path was drenched with cream and the rocks poured out olive oil...Whoever heard me spoke well of me...I put on righteousness as my clothing and justice was my robe and my turban."*

As the thoughts of glimmering times faded, Job grew in his frustration with God for how could someone who had led such a blessed and righteous life, now be considered a laughing stock by his friends and associates. Job still could not accept blame for his situation and demanded answers from God. Unable to stay silent any longer, Elihu, the youngest of the group of men puzzling over God's wisdom, spoke up.

Elihu said to Job: *"I heard the very words, I am pure, I have done nothing wrong, yet God finds fault with me...but I tell you, in this, you are not right for God is greater than any mortal...God does speak...though no one perceives it...He repays everyone for what they have done...Job speaks without knowledge and his words lack insight...to his sin he adds rebellion...If you sin how does that affect him?...Your wickedness or righteousness only affects humans like yourself…How much less then will he listen when you say that you do not see him…The one who has perfect knowledge is with you…If one is bound in chains…he tells them what they have done, they have sinned arrogantly…He is wooing you from the jaws of distress to a spacious place free of restriction, to the comfort of your table laden with the food of your choice…but now you are laden with judgement due to the wickedness…He does not have regard for any who think they are wise."*

After all the riddles and narration between the men, Job finally heard the Lord whose voice came to him out of the storm and spoke these words:

"Who is the one that obscures my plans with words without knowledge…Where were you when I laid the Earth's foundation, tell me if you understand…who shut the sea behind doors…have you ever given orders to the morning or shown dawn its place…Where is the way to the abode of light and where does darkness reside…The Ostrich….She lays her eggs on the ground…unmindful that a foot may crush them…she cares not that her labour was in vain… for God did not endow her with wisdom…Let him who accuses God, answer him."

Job utterly humbled by this wisdom that came from the Lord out of the storm said these things to the Lord:

"Surely I spoke of things I did not understand, things too wonderful for me to know…my ears had heard of you but now my eyes see you. Therefore I despise myself and repent in dust and ashes."

And with that, Job gained the wisdom of the mysterious ways in which the Lord can work. Despite the anger manifested around his three friends, Job forgave each one of them for speaking wrongly of the Lord and gave burnt offerings on their behalf. Once he had forgiven his friends, Job's healing began to take place and his wealth was restored beyond his imagination. He had seven sons and three daughters just as he had always had and lived to see four generations of grandchildren. When the time came, Job died peacefully in his sleep as an abundant man of many years and great wisdom.

The story of Job is given to us in riddles, left for those who have the patience to decipher the meaning.

At the start, we learn that Job is a man who fears God. He is what most in society would deem as an upright businessman, a family man and a religious man. He was quote on quote righteous. We also find out that Job was not entirely perfect as he would have paranoid thoughts about his children sinning without any evidence of them actually doing so. When the angels and Satan met with the Lord, we find that the ideas Job has about the Lord are not all he thought them to be. The term 'Lord' can also be understood as the Law because of the etymology. The Lord or the Law, as it will now be referred to, symbolises the natural laws that exist in all things beyond the scope of our imagination. These laws are the reason why the sun rises and sets every day. It is also the same reason why the stars come out at night, every cause has an effect and why our thoughts manifest into things.

The reason Satan was present when all of the angels went to see the Lord about Job, was because Satan had also been present in the mind of Job. Job had allowed Satan to cause a later effect in his life because his human mind was not completely pure in thoughts. Because of the Law, Satan was allowed to come into Job's life and deliver him four woes. Would he now still believe that he was a blameless man even though all his possessions, livelihood and children had gone?

In this initial test and moment of devastation, Job did not sin because he remained in an attitude of gratitude. Job worshipped the Lord for everything that had been given to him and for everything that had been taken away. Although Job had surrendered to his situation and remained upright in thoughts, Satan still lingered in the karma Job had made. Job was then struck down with illnesses so bad he could not eat and was bedridden. His skin peeling at the fire is a symbol of purging. By the Law of Job's thoughts, actions and karma, Job was submerged into the state of purging where he would have to reveal the truth about his thoughts. Something important to note is Job could not pass on to the next stage of his evolution until he had entered the mind of God by purging his old belief patterns. All had been taken from Job to induce this purging, all except his life. He would have to face his thoughts and belief systems before he could live, die or anything in between.

The three friends of Job represent this evolution of thought. Job had to bear witness to his old belief system through the words of his friends (sword and words can be used interchangeably in etymology). Each friend revealed an old thought pattern of Job which he then released through his long narratives. Job feels ashamed and embarrassed by the thoughts and so-called wisdom his friends brought to him, thoughts which were once his own.

The suffering and agony he endured showed that there were belief systems, mysteries and laws, way beyond what he understood. If he had not entered into the state of purging, he may have lived his entire life ignorant of this fact. Finally, Elihu, speaks. He is young and represents the rebirth of thoughts for Job. Importantly he says:

"Job speaks without knowledge and his words lack insight…to his sin he adds rebellion."

The 'sob story' Job had narrated to his friends showed that he lacked knowledge of the Law. Specifically, he lacked insight, meaning he had not yet seen the power behind creation. By speaking out his negative thoughts, he added rebellion to his lack of wisdom, which only kept him further away from the truth. When Elihu speaks, Job begins to reminisce about the days when he was in a state of gratitude. Those days of upright thoughts had brought hope to his life which supported all his success. This change in thoughts was the beginning of his transformation. It represents how a shift in our way of thinking can make us feel differently about our circumstances resulting in a change closer to our desired manifestations. Our thoughts should make us smile with joy and fill our minds with glory and hope. Our imagination should be filled with glittering dreams and splendid wonders so that we can work with 'the Law' of creation. Just as Job discovered, this realisation is not something that can be discussed and reasoned with academically. It is a realisation that must come from within, with a sense of 'seeing' the power of thoughts for our very self, so that we become aware of their power. Elihu also said:

"He is wooing you from the Jaws of distress to a place that is spacious and without restriction."

This part of the riddle is an invitation for Job to go into silent meditation so that he could release himself from the rigid thought patterns responsible for his suffering. Through meditation, you can consciously relax the mind so that higher wisdom can come in and reset thoughts that are not of service. Job finally hears the Lord in his meditation and comes to know that there are certain Laws that we can not understand with intellect alone. We must know that our thoughts are connected to the divine in ways our human minds can not understand.

Manifesting a dream life is not about being righteous, it is more about being in tune with the Law. You don't get what you deserve, you get what you focus on because in every thought karma is created. In the epilogue, we see that Job must forgive his three friends for the false knowledge they gave to him before he could be renewed. Forgiveness represents the mercy you must show to yourself when you get stuck in negative thought patterns. We are not always aware of our karma so when we find ourselves in undesirable situations, we must learn to forgive ourselves so that we can give ourselves space for the new self to be born.

Just like Job, this process of rejuvenating thoughts can come after a long period of being in a cycle of negative thoughts. When these mind attacks occur it is a great opportunity to forgive yourself and your beliefs that no longer serve you. Once you finally come into the silence residing behind the thoughts, the truth of your heart is revealed which elevates your being to a new level of conscious power and manifestation mastery.

6 Writing things down

Human beings have been passed a gift which has remained here on earth over many years of change and shifts in consciousness. This gift has withstood the test of time and is quoted in the bible for good measure. "In the beginning was the word...and the word was god." The gift I am speaking of, of course, is our innate ability to communicate with one another through language and the written word. Our language abilities are a part of our superpower as humans and are extremely sophisticated compared to other species on earth. This intrinsic form of communication, when used correctly, can be harnessed to attract and manifest the dreams which we desire.

One of the amazing talents that separate humans from other communicating creatures on this planet is our ability to use and comprehend the written word. I mean what other species of animal do you know that can sit and read a book on a Sunday afternoon for entertainment? Think about that closely for a second. We are the only species on this planet that can effectively and precisely communicate with one another through symbols, numbers and lettering.

When, for example, we can see a sign that says stop, we adjust our movements in such a way so that we do not get slammed by a car. We have at this moment used written language to semi-predict the future. Incredible don't you think? Maybe you never really thought about it that way before but I hope to reveal to you the intelligence and mystical magic that is behind the written and spoken word.

In the same way that we can use written language to make impressions on pedestrians, we can use the written word to make an impression on the All Consciousness. It is from this unseen consciousness that the gift of words and spelling comes. Let's look at how exactly the written word can make an impression on the unseen All Consciousness, so that we may manifest our desires.

Written words are spellings and spellings are spells. Whenever you write something down you are giving it physical form and casting a mystical, magical spell. Sounds a bit out of this world but at this point, you should be accustomed to unconventional ideologies. To better understand the science of why spellings are indeed real-life magical spells, let's look at the definition and etymology of 'spell'. The first, more conventional meaning is to: "write or name letters that give form to a word." Another valid definition is: " A form of words used as a magical charm or incarnation." This is an occult definition and although some may roll their eyes at this interpretation, the etymological meaning is the same for both. Both definitions tell you that by stringing a phrase of letters or words together in the correct order, they will give form to something. That something can be a word or sentence which gives commands and instructions to other people. That something can also be words or sentences which give form to the things we most desire, by giving commands and instructions to the natural mystic blowing in the wind. Either or, the root of the word 'to spell' is to tell another what to do.

To spell is to give form to something in a way that transforms the reader of those spellings. Not many are aware of why writing things down has such an impact on their manifestation. Many may not care to explore the god realms so that they may know, but ask a successful person, a master manifester, what are some of the tools they have used to accumulate their riches and they will tell you that there is a power in writing things down.

One example I love is that of Jim Carrey. At age 21, Jim Carrey was a broke, hopeless aspiring actor with big dreams of Hollywood life. In 1992 Jim wrote himself a cheque to be paid into his bank account for ten million dollars. In 1995 Jim received the good news that he would be starring in the hit movie 'Dumb and Dummer' for which he would be paid ten million dollars for his acting services. Jim Carrey gave form to his desires through the magical mystical technique of spelling. He gave a spell to his desires and moved through the sea of thoughts and prayers graciously. He moved through the ocean of consciousness faithfully knowing that he would arrive at his destination.

Spelling can also be a way of programming the mind through what is known as autosuggestion. Napoleon Hill writes about autosuggestion in his book 'Think and Grow Rich.'
An autosuggestion is essentially a form of self-hypnosis that works by feeding the subconscious mind with subtle symbols and signages. The repetitive viewing of these signs moulds the subconscious mind and the belief system of the individual to the point where they begin to expect to see the signage as a manifestation. The subconscious mind will begin to move the individual in a way so that their behaviour matches the frequency of the desired manifestation. Eventually, after enough signage repetition, matched with corresponding behaviours, the individual attracts what it is that they desire.

Autosuggestion can work simply by writing the desired manifestation down and viewing it at regular intervals. When Jim Carrey wrote his cheque for ten million dollars, he put it into his wallet and would take it out and look at it frequently until the day he eventually had the real thing in his grasp. This was a way for Jim to reprogramme his subconscious mind into believing without any doubts that the manifestation would one day become real. Because the subconscious mind works best through imagery, anything it sees, it absorbs. It then uses the images to create vivid images in the conscious mind. These daydreams and visuals give a strong wave of attraction toward you as the individual. It is through your imagination that the seeds of manifestation germinate.

So how can you manifest your desires and dreams simply by writing things down? The magic in spelling, or 'scripting' as some may call it, is extremely powerful and has worked for many successful individuals over and over again however, there is more to it than simply putting words to paper. Once the desire has been written down on paper, it is up to the individual to make it a habit of repetitively reviewing what has been written down. It is also important that the individual believes that they will have what it is that they are manifesting through spellings. Any doubts or fear when reviewing the writings will set a vibration away from you. You must write what it is that you want down and then believe in its obtainment wholeheartedly. You need to feel extremely grateful that it is on its way to you. It is this excitement and feeling of gratitude that will motivate you to perform the actions needed to bring about its physical manifestation.

Here are some practical techniques that you can use to begin successfully scripting. Firstly you want to make your spellings clear and legible. Use a black pen which will not smudge and paper which is a blank canvas. Take your time to write out what you want so that you can clearly read what has been written. You may choose to cast your spellings in capital letters so that your handwriting is clearer and easier to read. It is not entirely necessary to script using a black pen. Using a blue pen or a pencil is fine. The main objective is to make the spellings as clear to read as possible. If you like, you can use either a journal or a notepad to write down your manifestations. If you are writing in a journal, it is important to write in the present and past tense. The subconscious mind is not concerned about what may happen in the future. As far as it is concerned, whenever it sees something or a visualisation occurs in the imagination, that thing has already happened or is happening now. Because we know how the subconscious mind works, it is important to appeal to it when scripting. In your journal, you can write as if you are reflecting on your day. Give as much detail about the events that occurred as you can. For example, you can write something like.

"Dear universe, I am so grateful for the incredible day I had today. I went to the bank today full of joy, wearing my brand new red bottom designer shoes, the ones with the diamond embroidery. So many people smiled and gave their blessings to me as I passed by. Too many to remember but I acknowledge each of their smiling faces. When I arrived at the bank, I was greeted by a very friendly clerk who offered me a glass of champagne. I sipped the glass on a beautiful blue crushed velvet sofa where I waited to be seen. When I finished the delicious glass of French champagne, I made my way to the VIP lounge where I was offered another glass of champagne and a selection of herbal teas. I sat at the clerk's desk and after a moment of typing on her keyboard, with her long acrylic nails, she turned her computer screen towards me. The screen showed my checking account balance for today. There was a multi-digit figure with six zeros after it. Today I found out that I am a multi-millionaire and that all the money is available to me to spend as freely as I wish, for the valuable services I have rendered in 2022. I feel flooded with joy, satisfaction and gratitude as I accept this now as my truth. Forever grateful, Lorae Knight."

In this example, you can see the specific details that were visualised while writing this. It is important to go into as much detail as possible. You have to be very clear about the things you want and in what capacity, time and place they come to you. It is also very important to write down a date or a place in time that you desire the manifestation to happen. For example, you can script for the manifestation to come to you after you finished your exams or on a specific birthday. Now please understand that God/the universe/the great All Consciousness is extremely mystic in its ways. Just because you wrote down specific details does not guarantee that you will get everything right on time and just the way you want it. There is such a thing as divine timing however the details help to prevent you from receiving your asks in a way that is completely out of alignment with what it is that you truly desire. Focus on what your heart desires when scripting and not so much on what's in your head. This way even if you receive your manifestations in a way that you were not entirely expecting (which is usually the case) at least it will still be in alignment with your heart's true desires. PSA: remember the chapter on using the power of good? Most of us like to believe we have good hearts which are lighter than Maat's feather however, this isn't the case for the majority. You will receive the sweetest, strongest manifestations when you have done your 'shadow work' and cleaned up your heart vibration before scripting.

If you are not someone who likes to journal, then you can also try 'post-it note' scripting. On your sticky pad, write down the goals and desires you want. Try your best to write them in the present or past tense so that your subconscious mind begins to believe that you already have them. For example, you can write:

I am a billionaire,
I am in the best health I have ever been,
I am a loving and loved wife.

You can then post these notes in places where you will see them daily. Maybe your bathroom, your calendar or your office desk. The key is to subject your subconscious to repetition, so make sure you put them somewhere where you can see them regularly. You can also do something similar to what Jim Carrey did and write yourself a cheque and then put it somewhere so that you can see it at regular intervals. It doesn't have to just be a cheque. Why not write yourself a plane ticket and boarding pass. You might want to write yourself a congratulations letter for your dream job or a wedding invitation for your dream wedding with your dream partner. Whatever it is that you desire, you can begin to set a wave in your direction by writing it down.

Lastly, if you are more practical-minded, and not really into writing 'imaginary' letters to yourself, then you may want to script in the more traditional way of goal setting. To do this, write down the thing that your heart most desires. Put as much detail as you possibly can. You can even draw items and objects to add even more details. From here begin to think about what steps you would need to take so that you mechanically become closer to your desire. This process is called reverse engineering and can be done easily by asking yourself the five Ws + H.

Who, What, Why, When, Where and How.

Don't make this process complicated. Start where you are and with what you currently have available to you and go from there. As you begin to move closer to your goal, more things, people and places will come into your environment as tools to help you get your hands on your manifestation. An example may look like this: If you have the goal of moving to your dream destination, you will want to write the location, the specific city, the street name and then the date when you want to move by. You then ask yourself the five W's + H. So How? Okay, you're probably going to have to get a plane there right, so go look at prices for one-way tickets to your dream location and write that down. You now have a practical figure of how much you need to get there. Now ask yourself the five W's + H again. How will you get the money for the plane, who will help you get this money and why? When will you get this money and in what way will it come to you? Where will you be when you receive the money? Keep doing this for every aspect of your goal until you have a fully detailed, practical plan that you can begin putting into practice immediately. Don't take this exercise lightly. Writing things down to bring about their success is well known and well practised by practically anyone who has accumulated great success.

Writing is a sacred gift and its powers are deep-rooted in a deity known as Thoth/Tuhuti who is said to have brought writing to earth beings many millennia ago. In 52,000 BC, an Atlantean priest-king named Tuhuti was swept up on the shores of Khem. Tuhuti, along with several thousand refugees had just escaped a devastating flood which had

completely devoured their civilisation. When Tuhuti and his
kinsmen arrived on the banks east of their once native lands,
they were met with spears and the raging roars of African
barbarians attempting to protect their land from foreign
invaders. Tuhuti dismounted his ship and came before the
fierce fighters. With just one pound of his staff on the wet
sandy ground, Tuhuti sent a powerful wave of cosmic energy
toward the African warriors. The wrath of the wave
perplexed the warriors and immediately they stopped their
ambush. As still as stone, the warriors froze in their tracks
and dropped their weapons before the humbled priest-king.
Gently and with a voice as calm as a slumbering baby, Tuhuti
explained that he and his kinsmen did not come as invaders
but as refugees from a disaster which had occured in distant
lands.

He explained to them that before he had been washed of
everything, he had been a master of wisdom. From a young
age, Tuhuti was taught the ancient ways by his father who
was a guardian of the great holy temple in Atlantis. Seeing
that his son had a fierce fascination for wisdom and near
enough nothing else, he taught Tuhuti all the ways of the
gods who dwelled among their people in the temples. For
many years, Tuhuti studied the great mysteries of darkness
and light under the profound teaching of his father. His
dedication to the attainment of powerful knowledge was that
of no other before him and this did not go unnoticed by the
great gods who dwelled deep within the temples.

At last, it came the day when Tuhuti's commitment to
understanding the power of the light was to be
commemorated. The great god who dwelled at the heart of

the temple called for Tuhuti to come before him, something which only a handful of others had done and lived to tell the tale. The great god who dwelled in the temple could see that the light of wisdom shone brightly in Tuhuti and so it was deemed that the great mysteries of the light would be revealed to him. When Tuhuti stood in the light of truth, its burning eternal flame consumed him but he was not burnt. Seeing that his heart was pure, the god who dwelled in the temples of Atlantis summoned him to become a guardian of the temple. This temple becomes Tuhuti's home for many years and many ages of wisdom.

Deep within the temples, Tuhuti learned many mysteries of space and time. He learned to travel to the stars and how to stop time. He learned about the underworld and the eternal god who dwelled there. He learnt about life and death until he reached a point of immortality, free to come and go on this plane as he pleased. Tuhuti had become so close to becoming one with the eternally burning fire that lives within all but there was a mystery that lay deep in the heart of man that kept his burning desire for knowledge alive.

And then the day of the great flood came and with its great might, devoured the whole of Atlantis. Tuhuti was instructed by the gods of the Temple to take his kinsmen in a substantial ship and sail to the land of Khem. Here the last survivors of Atlantis would live for many generations, fulfilling the purpose of the eternal one. Tuhuti ruled over Khem for many generations, bringing to the land many magnificent wonders. He taught the children of men about chemistry (the magic science) and how to obtain and retain knowledge. He assembled the great pyramid, putting over them a gravity-defying crystal which sanctioned time travel to and from the underworld. He taught the sons of man all about mathematics and sacred geometry. Yes, Tuhuti brought many magical ways to Khem so that they rose to become a noble nation.

Of all the sacred gifts Tuhuti brought, the most important of them was the gift of writing. Writing gave the children of man the tools to preserve the wisdom they had gained in the form of records, books and hieroglyphics. Tuhuti was best known for giving the gift of writing and languages to the children of men. The wisdom of his teachings meant that the people of Khem could 'cast spells' simply by stringing the correct phrase of words together, resulting in instantaneous manifestations.

For 16,000 years, Tuhuti was considered a god amongst men in ancient Egypt and the papyrus was his greatest attribute. Because of Tuhuti's wisdom and teachings in writing, those men who could afford it would have a 'Book Of The Dead' written for them. This sacred text gave man divine instructions on how to pass through into the underworld, just as freely as Tuhuti, once they were deceased.

In 32,000 BC, Tuhuti took on his third and final incarnation in the land of Khem. Once his incarnation was complete he returned to the place far beneath, where the flame of eternity burnt endlessly at the core of the earth. Before he left, Tuhuti gave one final gift to man so that they may always remember the wisdom that he had shown them. Tuhuti sourced 10 infant-sized tablets made of pure emerald. In them, he carved instructions on how to obtain great wisdom. He chose to write the instructions in ancient Atlantean and constructed the words in such a way that anyone who set their eyes upon them would instantaneously be enlightened by their inscription. The power of the inscription was so strong that enlightenment even came to those readers who didn't understand the exact words written upon them. Before departing, he instructed the pyramid priests to guard the tablets with their life and to give their descendants the duty of guarding them for generations to come. Tuhuti then blasted a passageway from the earth's crust deep into the earth's core. Darkness was the only way into the underworld, and only those pure of heart and with the divine wisdom written upon the emerald tablets could dare follow him.

It is said that Tuhuti will incarnate on earth once again at a time when man has turned his heart inward once more. It is during this time that people will be more focused on seeking knowledge and truth than they are on Netflix and chilling. Although the story of Tuhuti can sometimes be viewed as a legend, the main takehome from his mysterious existence is that writing and spelling have for many aeons been deemed to be something out of this world. The written word is a mystical gift bestowed onto human civilization as a way to harness wisdom. It is through wisdom that alchemy, enlightenment and divine manifestation can be cultivated. Although the languages we use today are diluted in their power and may not carry the potency of ancient Atlantean, the fact that we can still speak languages and write in various texts is because of a divine entity who gifted us with such a tool. Use it wisely to nurture your dreams.

7 DESIRE

Anything that came to be on earth first started with a burning desire to see, taste, touch, feel and hear its manifestation. Desire is what makes the sun rise and set every day. It is what makes the seeds, planted deep below in the earth's soil break through to the surface. Desire is the screaming newborn, whose voice never goes hoarse and who never quits hollering until their dissatisfaction is satisfied. Depending on what action is taken after it comes, desire can either painfully consume an individual or it can propel them forward into timely action and bring about forces for divine manifestation.

Of all the principles written about manifesting, desire may be the most important. Without a strong and definite desire for something to happen the chances of it happening are completely up to the winds. If you are learning to be a master manifester, you need to know that your passion for something to exist is the foundation block for bringing it about. It is desire itself that is said to have initiated the beginning of existence. It is the big bang, the god force which causes the continuous need for expansion. Without desire, you and I would not exist.

The key thing to be noted is that the term desire carries an element of intensity with it. When you desire something, you want it with every cell of your body. It haunts your existence and drives you into consistent and persistent action. Even if something is unseen or on a surface level appears unlikely to be possible, a fiery hunger can override every single doubt. Desire is spoken about in many religious texts and philosophised by many great minds. One principle that is consistent when desire is spoken about is the magnitude of its expression. To give an illustration, I will use a quotation from the bible:

"I know your deeds, that you are neither cold nor hot. I wish you were either one or the other! So, because you are lukewarm—neither hot nor cold—I am about to spit you out of my mouth."- Revelations 3:15-16.

Here the archangel of Laodicea, speaks to its congregation and communicates to them that their desire must be pure. This is not to say that it must be righteous of intent but that it must be extremely polarised to bring about its existence. This means that there can be no doubt in one's mind about the realisation of the thing that one wishes to manifest. If you say that you want to be wealthy, you can not in the same breath also speak of things that indicate that you also wish to be broke. If you want to be married, you can not in the same breath also wish things onto yourself which indicates that you also wish to be single. If you wish to have a child, you can not also ask for things to come into your existence which will make you barren. Your desire must not consist of any doubts contradictory to its nature.

To not be passionate about the things you want in life means that you are lukewarm. Lukewarm desires do not possess the god force power which can bring about all things imaginable from out of the ether. What can anyone do with a limp pillar of passion? It certainly is not going to impress your counterpart, nor is it going to penetrate the realms of beings where all things created and not yet created exist.

Can we then agree that to have desire means to be 100% sure of what it is that you want. It is to be fully embedded in the feeling of possessing what it is that you want. Once you have established what your desire is, the god force can decipher the things that you do want and the things which you do not want. It can therefore begin to move in a way that is harmonious to your polarities of desire.

So how do you know what it is that you want and what you do not want? This would seem a simple enough question but in my experience and observation of many beings in this current world, many of us do not know what we want. Most think that they know what they want however actually most are simply lukewarm. It only takes a moment of honest questioning to find out what someone's true desires are. For example, you might ask someone if they would like a lot of money. Most people would answer yes to this question. However if you ask them how much they would like and what they would do with the money, most will not have a definite answer.

It may be true when you ask this question that the recipient responds that they would like a lot of money so that they can buy a nice house, nice car and live comfortably and maybe give some of it away to charity. This response is lukewarm.

The recipient of the question does not desire a lot of money, for if they did they would already know specifically what for and specifically how much. They would flood the conversation with details and even plans on how they expect to acquire the money. The person who responds that they desire a lot of money so that they may live a comfortable life does not truly desire a lot of money, they just like the idea of it.

Similarly, you may ask a person if they desire peace in their lives. Many will say yes they desire peace however when you observe the toxic people, situations and temperaments of these types of people, you will see that actually, they desire chaos. A person who desires peace will find peaceful practices. Maybe they will often go on a digital detox or meditate regularly. The person who desires peace will spend a lot of time in nature and want to be surrounded by light giving beings. A person who says they want peace but never leaves the busy city or still screams down the phone to their toxic ex doesn't desire peace. This type of person only enjoys the idea of having peace and any conversations around the desired state is merely a fantasy.

Beyond asking questions and observing our behaviours, we can also establish what our desires are by listening to our emotions and discerning our feelings. You will know if you truly want something by the feeling that it gives you when you think of it. Your truest, most passionate desires can be likened to the feeling of thinking about a lover. No matter what you do, they are always there in the back, front and centre of your mind. When you focus your attention on them, a wave of joy washes across your face and instantly a smile is placed there. You might also dream about your lover or be in a state of serendipity, where you see the object of desire everywhere you go. If you find yourself feeling down, you want to focus your attention on them and immediately feel light and expansive. You want to tell everyone in the whole wide world about the desire burning deep within, which is ready to burst out.

In contrast, if you feel sadness, frustration, anger, pain or fear, then you have no desire for the thing which currently has your attention. Your feelings are a fantastic navigation tool that points you in the direction of truly knowing yourself. It is your responsibility to become the master of your feelings. When I say become the master of your feelings, I do not mean repressing your feelings or to show no emotions. Please do not do this.

To become a master of your feelings, you must first be aware of them and where they have come from. If every time you see your spouse you feel anger and frustration towards them, you are expressing to the god force that you do not desire them as a spouse any longer. The god force, who works in mysterious ways alongside our feelings, will then begin to put things into your existence so that you no longer are with your spouse. Some in this situation may say, 'it is not that I do not desire my spouse why I feel anger towards them but because they have acted in such a way that I do not appreciate.' This simply means that your spouse has acted in a way that goes against the desires you have for a partner. As a master of your feelings and desires, it is important to observe why the particular act of your partner made you put a force in motion away from them. Are your desires ones that need to be met outside of a relationship or is your spouse completely unable to meet your interpersonal needs? If it is the latter, then it is likely true that actually you do not desire your spouse but are simply remaining with them out of comfort.

Your feelings are telling you that you are uncomfortable not having your interpersonal desires met. If you remain lukewarm about what you truly want, you are not able to let your true desires come to you. It is important, to be honest with yourself.

Lying to yourself about what it is your heart truly desires will only bring about hardships and situations which bring about intense contrast between what you passionately want and what you truly do not want. This contrast occurs so that you can observe your emotions and make a decision. Whenever you experience hard times and tough emotions, it's like the universe/the god force, is screaming at you "WHAT THE HELL DO YOU WANT? LET ME KNOW SO THAT I CAN BRING IT TO YOU ALREADY!"

The god force can only understand the desires of the heart. It has no concept of societal programmes or ego. It has no concept of material gains or items perceived by others that once obtained, deem you as being a worthy human being. The only thing the god force knows is what you express to it through clear intense desires. The desires that truly match your heart are communicated to the god force through joy, love and passion. We can often get sidetracked by our emotions, personal life and distractions from our environment; causing the god force to delay gratifications. To fully understand what it is that you want, the god force may dangle temptations and symbols of your desires in front of you so that it may test your heart before giving it to you. It needs to be sure that what you desire also desires you. When you are presented with the thing you say your heart desires, the god force is observing your emotions to know if you are a vibrational match. Do you get excited when you see the thing that you desire happening for others? Does your heart amplify the images presented to you? You may indeed begin to see your desires more and more just before you manifest them for yourself. It can feel like the universe is teasing you but it is just making sure that your heart truly is a match for the things you say you desire before delivering it to you.

It is also very important to note here that we must not, by any means, get caught up by things which come into our environment which are not a vibrational match to our desires, as they cause us to experience unpleasurable emotions. Experiencing things which we do not desire is a part of the dual universe we are currently living in. It is crucial to recognise that experiencing what we desire and experiencing what we do not desire are ultimately the same thing. Both emotions of passion and excitement or frustration and disappointment all point to what it is that you truly want. So when you begin to feel intense negative emotions, turn your attention to your heart and just say 'thank you.' Give gratitude to your heart for showing you what you don't want and for providing a clear and intense contrast of what you don't want so that you can have better clarity and focus on what you do want. Do not rave and rage over something that has happened to you which is not in alignment with what you want, as the god force can easily mistake this passionate rage for emotions of desire.

Remember the god force communicates with us through passionate feelings and will bring about whatever is attached to these feelings, whether hot or cold. When you have experienced what you do not desire, observe the contrast and accept the experience but then immediately begin visualising and listening to your heart about what it is that you do want. Is it not true that if you experience something that you don't want, you are in contrast or direct opposition to the thing that you do want? Focus on that. You, as a master manifester, can transmute your feelings into direct communication with the god force so that it can know specifically what it is that you want. Once it knows clearly what you want it can then bring it to you in a timely fashion and without the obstacles of doubt that we create in our minds.

The final point to make here will help you to have certainty over what it is that you desire. Your desires are merely a reflection of who you currently believe and are expressing yourself to be. For example, if you are a student, you will have a desire to ace your exams. If you claim yourself as single, you may have the desire to be in a relationship. If you are depressed, you may desire to experience happiness. Your desires are a clear reflection of who you believe yourself to be at this moment.

When you recognise this statement to be true, you have greater power to attract your true desires. Some desires you may have can cause you to remain in a past paradigm because of the belief you have about yourself. For example, if you desire to be wealthy however you are focused on just having enough money to pay off your credit card debts, then you are telling the god force that you are bad with money rather than someone wealthy. If your primary focus on riches is simply to get out of debt, even if you clear those debts, it is only a matter of time before you will begin spending on the credit card once more. If you desire to be wealthy, it is vital that you feel you already are. You must programme your subconscious mind into becoming the person you already believe yourself to be.

Once you believe yourself to be, right now, the person who you most desire to be, you will begin to have desires which directly reflect that person. For example, a luxury car owner may start to have desires of buying a new keyring for the car that they are going to buy next. They may start to have the desire of going to the car dealership and test driving their future car. They may even have the desire to browse through the catalogue of luxury cars with an imagination that formulates a plan of how they will acquire one.

As a master manifester, it is very important to be aware of your thoughts, feelings and desires. Always in your mind's eye, be the person who you wish to be. Even when everything around you suggests you are anything but that person, your feelings should always reflect your desired state. Block out the noise and opinions of others who only see the exterior of who you are. When you are saying to yourself, I want this, I need this, why isn't this here yet. Ask yourself are these the wants and needs of the person I desire to be or are they a reflection of my past self? What is it that your heart truly desires? Become hot about what it is that you want and cold about what it is that you do not want. Never sit in between. Use your feelings to guide you into knowing what your true feelings are. If you feel joy, excitement and happiness when you experience the expression of something desirable to you, then you are on the right path to attracting it. If you feel frustration, anger or disappointment about something you are currently experiencing, then you are also on the right path. This is true just so long as you use these cold emotions to give you contrast and clarity over what it is that your heart truly desires. Do not dwell in the place of disappointment. Use this energy to drive you into actions which bring about your truest desires.

In 2150 BC Abram, son of Terah, was born into the land of Ur of Chaldeans. Abram had two brothers and his wife was called Sarai. Sarai was a woman of stunning beauty. Everywhere that she would go, people would compliment just how much her regal looks resembled those of popular princesses. Although it was true that Sarai was fragrantly feminine and boldly beautiful, after several years of marriage she was still yet to bear a child for Abram.

Abram and Sarai's longing for a child of their own burned a hole of deep desire for parenthood in their hearts. As a result, Abram would spend many moments in the presence of god praying to be blessed with an heir. God told Abram to have faith in the Lord and to listen to his instruction. He told him that as long as he stayed faithful to the Lord, his wife Sarai would bear him a child.

Abram was then told by God to take his elderly father, Terah, along with his wife Sarai and move from Ur to a faraway land called Canaan. As appeasement for their longing to be parents, Abram's nephew, Lot, went with them on their travels under their parental guidance. The journey was long and laborious, especially for Terah who was frail and feeble.

The travellers ended up taking refuge in Harran, where they settled for many years and where Terah was eventually laid to rest.

The event of his father's death only made Abram more aware of his own mortality. He desired more desperately a legacy in the form of an heir. Abram spoke to god, as he frequently did, about his desires and God promised to him that he would be a great prosperous nation with a name that would be known far and wide. All his desires were promised to him so long as he remained faithful to the Lord. Abram listened to god's instructions.

At age 75, Abram took his wife, his servants, his nephew and all their possessions out of Harran and began their journey of many miles to the land of Canaan. When Abram arrived in Canaan his heart was filled with faith and he heard the voice of God tell him that the land where he stood would be given to his offspring. Feeling accomplished and nearer to his destiny, he thanked God and built an altar of worship therein dedication to the omnipotent spirit to whom he was faithful.

When famine hit the land of Canaan, God told Abram to follow his instructions for he would make him prosperous and wealthy; unlike the fate of many who were to remain in Canaan. So Abram took Sarai and Lot and headed to Egypt. When they arrived in Egypt, Abram observed the land and knew that they would stand out as foreigners. Not only were they dressed and cultured differently but Sarai's phenomenal beauty would surely draw unwanted attention to them.

Afraid of what might happen to him if they found out that such an extraordinary woman was his wife, Abram told Sarai to pretend that she was his sister. By pretending to be his sister, should anyone wish to pursue Sarai they would have to gain Abram's favour; instead of trying to kill him if they knew she was actually his wife.

The plan worked. When they arrived in Egypt, the guardsmen told word to Pharaoh of the foreign travellers and the beauty of Sarai. Pharaoh sent for Sarai so that he may know of her beauty. When he saw her, he confirmed that the rumours were true and took Sarai to live in his court as his wife. Thinking that Abram was Sarai's brother, Pharaoh sent him many gifts and fortune. Soon Abram had enough wealth to live very comfortably for the rest of his days while also being free from malicious attacks by Pharaoh. After some time, a plague broke out in the household of Pharaoh and in a message from God, Pharaoh was told that the disease had come to curse him because he had taken another man's wife. Pharaoh could see then that Abram and Sarai were favoured by God and sent them on their way with all their possessions, never touching a single hair on their heads.

Abram eventually returned to Canaan and acquired innumerable riches and land. His riches were so grand that he had to part from his nephew Lot so that their sheep and cattle had enough land to graze. When Abram finally settled in Canaan with all his riches, he sat down in the presence of God and thanked him. Abram thanked God for the legacy he had accumulated; however, it was still true that his burning desire to have a child lived in the centre of his heart.

His desire burned even more furiously now that he had parted from Lot and now that he had so much abundance to give but no family to give it to. Abram heard God tell him to lay his eyes upon the land of Canaan. He heard God say that he would make his offspring like the individual grains of sands which made up the dust in the land in which he had settled. After hearing this message Abram felt reassured and hopeful that he would eventually have a child with his wife Sarai and in his faith, he built an altar for god in the land which had been promised to his offspring.

Abram remained in Canaan for many years with Sarai and although they gained great favour with the kings who accompanied the surrounding lands, they remained childless. In his frustration, Abram went out in the night and vented to God. He cried that all the riches, all the status and the protection that God had given to him were meaningless since he still had not received the very thing that he had always desired; a child that he could love and leave his estate to. He complained that he would have to give all he had inherited from God to one of his servants seeing as he had no heir to give it to. He deemed all he had done in his life meaningless. When God heard the cries of Abram, he told him to look to the stars and count them. Abram heard God say that he would not need to leave his estate to his servant for his offspring would be as many as the stars in the sky. Abram accepted this message from God and made a sacrifice in honour of it.

Sarai's heart grew into great sorrow watching her husband spend his days in dismay, for the fact that he had no son or even daughter to whom he could give all the treasures of his life. Despite how much faith he had put in God, Sarai, couldn't help but feel that his sorrow was largely her doing. She desired so much for her husband to have an heir, even if that heir did not come through her. Sarai went to Abram and told him to sleep with her slave, Hagar, so that she may conceive a child that they could then raise together as their own. Abram agreed to what Sarai suggested and so took Hagar as his wife.

After a short time, Hagar became pregnant and it seemed that the prophecy of God had been fulfilled. Abram was overjoyed that what he had seemingly been wanting all these years was finally coming to pass. Abram made sure that Hagar was well taken care of during her pregnancy, for surely the son that she carried held all the promises that God had given unto Abram. Becoming accustomed to the luxurious treatment she was receiving, Hagar began to overstep her mark and became resentful toward Sarai. She began to treat Sarai as if she was an unwanted mistress and so pain and jealousy began to grow in the heart of Sarai. When she expressed her feelings to her husband, Abram at once told Sarai that she was free to do as she pleased with her servant Hagar; as it was Sarai who had permitted Abram to take Hagar as their surrogate in the first place.

With Abram's blessing, Sarai denounced Hagar's position as his second wife. Sarai then confined Hagar to inadequate quarters, where she would remain in isolation for the duration of her pregnancy. Depression took over Hagar as the weeks went by, until a time when she couldn't take it anymore. She fled from the household of Abram out into the desert. While she was searching for water, an angel came to her and told her to return to her home with Sarai and Abram. The spirit of God reassured her that her son would be a strong, self-sufficient man who would be blessed with many descendants and so she decided to name her son Ishmael.

Just a few months after this incident, Ishmael was finally born. He was the first son of Abram and Abram was 86 years old when Ishmael arrived. For thirteen years, peace lived in the home of Abram and Sarai, for Ishamael had brought with him the satisfaction of a desire fulfilled. Although it had not come in the way that they had both expected, Abram's heart was content with the heir that had been gifted to him and Sarai was happy knowing that her husband's desire for a son had been gratified.

On a night when all the stars aligned, God came into the mind of Abram with the premise to establish a covenant between them. God was pleased with the heart of Abram and for the faithfulness that he had shown throughout the years. For this faithfulness, God promised Abram that he would give the land of Canaan to his descendants and that the messiah would come from the bloodline of himself and Sarai. God told Abram that he would from now on be known as Abraham, the father of great nations and Sarai would be known as Sarah meaning princess of noble stature. Abraham laughed in disbelief that he at age 100 and Sarah at age 90 would conceive a son, but God assured him that this was the prophecy. So long as Abraham kept his covenant that every male in his household would be circumcised, Sarah would give birth to a son the following year as promised. Abraham took his faith in the lord and ran with it. That very same day, he, Ishmael and all the males in his household were circumcised.

Abraham did not tell Sarah of his agreement with God as he thought that she would only dismiss him and call him a fool to believe that she at the dear age of 90 could ever have a son. She was well past the age of conceiving and the desire of having a child of her own had reduced down to ambering coal; a bleak fire which he did not want to reignite for her suffering.

One day, while Abraham was relaxing in the shade of the trees, three visitors of honourable stature appeared on the horizon before them. Recognising that they were men of the prophecy, Abraham invited them to stay the evening to rest and enjoy the company of his household. The visitors agreed and Sarah and her servants prepared the visitors a meal. As the three men enjoyed their food, Sarah overheard one of the men say that she would conceive and give birth to a son by the time they would return the next year. Sarah laughed at the thought of her, at such an elderly age, giving birth to a child but then she heard the supreme voice of God ask her why she laughed in disbelief. Did she not know that the god she served was capable of anything? Sarah became fearful and tried to redeem herself from the doubt by holding onto her faith in God.

Before long, Sarah became pregnant at 90 years of age and the following year gave birth to a son who she nursed herself.

Overwhelmed with joy and exhilaration that her deepest desire had finally been fulfilled, she said:

"God has brought me laughter and everyone who hears of this will laugh with me."

And so she named her son Isaac.

The story of Abraham and Sarah is so profound because it illustrates just what faith and desire combined can do. Although many doubted that Sarah and Abraham could ever have a child together, including themselves, the desire that burned deep in the very core of their being allowed for the wish to be fulfilled. It was a desire that kept Abraham up, praying to the stars at night and a desire which gave Sarah grace to allow her husband to sleep with and take her slave as his wife.

Their desire for a child spurred them to leave all they had known for many years and travel to distant lands where they stood out as foreigners and could have been killed. At times there were doubts in their mind about what it was they were doing and whether it was even possible to have their desires met. Still, their desire lived on as a certainty and their undying wish eventually gave them the gift that they had spent the majority of their life praying for.

8 KRIST PRINCIPLE

Within us all lives a divine being, whose birthright is to become and possess anything which its enchanting imagination can create. We all are born into this earth as children of God. Whether you believe in a deity or not, reclaim your power and accept this statement as truth.

This concept of being children of God can often be referred to as the Christ or Krist principle. To give clarity to this statement, I will refer to the story of Jesus Christ. Jesus Christ is a symbolic embodiment of the Krist principle. Jesus came onto earth by being born to "virgin" Mary. I must point out that the term virgin, does not mean that Mary had never had sex. It simply means that was childless and was of childbearing age. That being said, she was given a message that a child would be born to her through the process of divine conception. Through divine conception, the child's father would be God and so the child, Jesus, would inherit the genes and abilities of a god. The conception and birth of Jesus Christ should not be taken so literally but more symbolically to convey a message that there is a piece of divinity pulsing through our veins right now as we receive this teaching.

Just so we are clear, it is not only Christians who have portrayed these messages hidden in symbolism. The ancient Kemetic story of Horus and his falcon eye gives light to the Krist principle, which is the divinity of God residing in you.

Horus is the son of the sky god Osiris and Osiris is a deity associated with the sun and the underworld. In a battle with his uncle, Horus's left eye was snatched out. Thoth/Tuhuti offered to restore the left eye of Horus and return it to its proper place however Horus decided to sacrifice his eye and have it placed on the forehead of his father. The sacrifice of his eye allowed Osiris to see life on earth while remaining in the underworld, therefore opening him up to another level of consciousness through his 'third eye'. The symbolism within the story of the eye of Horus is directly related to the sixth sense or intuition available to us as human beings. The image of the eye is also related to the pineal gland, which possesses properties that activate our intuition, allowing us to see that which is hidden. The Krist principle exists in other religions and ancient mythologies, such as Hinduism, which we will go into more detail about later.

Whether you are religious or not, the point to take away here is that the Krist principle is a common teaching across many different cultures. The message is that residing within us all is a veiled version of God longing to be given expression. It is our responsibility to tap into the Krist within us, the eye of God, and do what we can here on earth so that our physical material world reflects the invisible 'underworld' where the father/God resides.

You may want to read over these concepts again so that you can fully grasp what is truly being said here. When you came to a comprehensive understanding, you will realise that your life is a joyous game and celebratory offering to the 'father' who has given you life here on earth. Let's take a moment to think about this. What did you do to deserve to come to this beautiful garden of Eden called earth? Nothing. Your heart beats faithfully for you, your breath is taken every moment without you even having to think about it. You get to laugh, dance, cry and overcome. You were nurtured and given enough education to read these words, which are revealing the hidden divinity within you. Life is a complete miracle and no one, not even the greatest of scientists can accurately explain how it is that we came to be. If we are to give wholehearted gratitude to the God force which sustains our life, we must become master manifesters. That is your only purpose. You must create a life for yourself which is so admirable and so pleasing to live that it makes your heart smile with satisfaction.

Think of it this way. The God force lives in heavenly realms not physically accessible to you. In contrast, God can not live as a physical human. You cannot enter one another's worlds however through the Krist principle, you can experience life together as one. You experience life together by communicating through the Krist principle, which is also your third eye. Through the images in your mind, created by your third eye, you are seeing what God sees. Through the emotions felt in your heart, God is feeling what you feel. To tell God what it is you would like to manifest from heaven onto earth, use your imagination and vividly paint a picture with the details of your truest desires. To communicate to the God force that you want more of anything, express joy and gratitude in your heart so that the force can be free to create abundantly on earth through your emotions. The key to this principle is that you and the God force are living as one and are mirroring your realities through images and emotions. As above, so below. Thy will be done on earth, as it is in heaven.

We go through our lives with programmes of a list of things that we have to accomplish by a certain age or a legacy that we must leave behind before we die. These societal concepts however are not the reality of what we are truly here to do. Your only responsibility on this earth is to create your version of heaven by becoming a master manifester. You are here to make your heart smile by successfully manifesting your heart's desires and in doing so, you return to your true nature which is oneness with the divine. When you embrace this concept, life becomes a lot easier and a lot more fun! In addition, once you can recognise the subtle yet supreme power that lies within the Krist principle, you become a powerful manifester and will begin to see yourself doing all the things in life that you always dreamt of.

So how can we recognise the Krist within? For the majority, embodying the Krist principle will not be a simple process. It is an ongoing journey and is going to require discipline and reprogramming of the mind. To use the Krist principle to manifest the harmonious and luscious life you have always dreamt of is to become one with the divine. Frankly, you are already one with the divine, you are very much already the embodiment of the Krist. The problem is you are the victim of a profound and irrevocable amnesia that is almost impossible to wake up from without physically leaving your body. You truly believe that you are you. That you are your body, you are your mind and you are all the things that you have unknowingly or intentionally created in your life. You are walking around in a human avatar where everything outside of yourself seems to be separate from you when in reality all is you. All that you observe in your reality is simply a reflection of the Krist you who you have left dormant and asleep in your vessel for the entirety of your conscious life.

To use the Krist principle as a sensational sixth sense, you must begin to do the work. You can begin this work in three ways:

1. Engaged detachment.
2. Embracing oneness.
3. Coming into the divine.

The first technique, engaged detachment, is all about removing your expectations of the outcome of desires without losing faith that you can manifest what it is that your heart craves. For example, a person may decide that it is within their heart's desire to get a job that allows them to work remotely and pays them more than their previous job. They apply for several jobs that would not only boost their status, give them a decent salary and pay them more than their last job, but also allows them to work from home but with occasional trips to the office. They decide that this would be the best option for them and they put all their desires and expectations of being successful in this role. They go to the interview and give it their best. A couple of weeks later they receive the news that they were turned down for all of the roles. For the person who is still operating as their human avatar and possesses a need to control every specific detail of their life, they will experience debilitating disappointment. They will ignore the email of rejection, accept that they will never make their dreams of working remotely come true, go back to their day job and never speak of the matter again. Now for the person who has begun to practice engaged detachment, they will be able to express gratitude for the rejection as they realise that this is divine intervention moving them closer to what they want. They detach from the outcome yet transmute the once perceived disappointing experience to one that brings them closer to the desired reality. They reply to the email expressing gratitude and continue to hold the desire of working remotely for decent pay in their heart. Six months later, the person receives an email from the same employer stating that they loved their attitude so much and that a role for another job has opened up which will offer more pay and more freedom to work remotely as they choose to. The role starts in a week and it is there available for them to start if they so wish. This is the Krist principle at work. It is the sheer belief that no matter what the current situation looks like, your will will be done.

The second technique is embracing oneness. This technique is simply to become aware that you are not separate from anything outside of yourself. Everything in your reality is a mirror of who you truly are. Everything. Even the things which are ugly and undesirable to you, those too are a part of who you are. You must accept wholeheartedly that you are the creator of everything you perceive. Without you, nothing exists. Your perception of something existing makes it so. Even very famous quantum physicists have theorised these ideas. It is your observation of something real that makes it that way. This means that at any given moment anything in our reality has the opportunity to become whatever it is that we decide it to be. We must come to recognise, without any doubt, that everything is in perfect harmony with our being. The more that we come into recognition of who we truly are, the more we will begin to bring peaceful and desirable situations into our lives. The more we change our perspective to one which perceives all things, even a blade of grass, as a mirror of ourselves the more we can embrace oneness. We have lived for many years under the illusion that we are separate from one another, even separate from God but in reality, you and the God force are one. It is only your perception of the illusion of separation which makes it so.

One way to begin to feel your mind-body being as oneness to diminish this veil of illusion is to practice yoga and meditation techniques which focus on bringing the being into recognition with the divine. When you silence the mind and melt into the sensation of nothingness, you can reach a point of stillness where you become one with the mind of the divine. This is a place within where you lose a sense of identity and begin to feel as if you are all things in the room in which you lay and all things beyond even this. To embrace this technique, I have uploaded a guided meditation on youtube which can be found here:

https://youtu.be/CFeNeZTofE4

The third and final technique to embodying the Krist principle is coming into the divine. To come into the divine is the realisation that there is no coming or going. You are already one with the divine as you are and have always been your divine self. This recognition is like shaking off lifelong amnesia. The amnesia itself made you forget that everything happening in the 'real' world is happening in the divine dream state simultaneously. Coming into the divine is to go on a journey with yourself. It will not simply happen overnight, except in rare cases.

It is often said that there are only two emotions experienced by humans, fear and love. All other emotions sit within the spectrum of these two. The divine, however, knows that there is only one emotion, which is unconditional love. Unconditional love is the God force energy which brings everything into existence. When you dust off the sleep from your eyes and begin to stretch your tired mind-body out of the constraints that it has been moulded to for many years, your perspective will shift and you will come to see this truth. When you wake up, you will see that everything you want and everything you need is already right here with you now. Even the blockages and barriers that your sleep self has put up over the years will be perceived as tools that the divine you can use to confirm that you have always been the one who you desire to be.

Please note that you can not become the divine as such. To become the divine, you need to feel yourself already as it. How can you begin to feel like the divine being you have always been? Well, you can start by taking a back seat in your life and allow the form to take place. Can you watch the story of your life play out like a movie without attaching it to anything or anyone in the storyline, including your human self? Can you sense the blissful harmony coming from your God aura in all that you do? Can you observe a situation and watch it from a place of unconditional love? When you begin to live as the divine you will be the master observer of harmony in your life. Every situation, even the adverse ones will become confirmations that you are moving closer to what it is that you desire to see in your story. You will be thankful in all moments, even the tough ones. To describe how to be divine and how to 'become' is a tricky concept to explain as its subtle spell is one of an experiential quality rather than a phenomenon that can be objectively described. When you come into the divine you become the master manifester. You will notice how any situation can come into your favour just by changing your perspective to that of unconditional love. Fear will begin to cease from your existence while situations and things will come to you seamlessly as you work on your manifestations. To be the divine within the human condition is the ultimate key to happiness and a fulfilling life.

For millions of people on the planet, there is one being by the name of Krishna believed to be the eighth complete incarnation of the most divine, the supreme god, Vishnu. In 3228 BC Devaki, sister of the evil tyrannical King Kamsa, gave birth to a son named Krishna whose skin was darker than the ocean at midnight and whose sparkling starry eyes mirrored those of lord Vishnu. Having prophesied that one of Devaki's children would end his life, King Kamsa locked Devaki and her husband away in a prison and demanded that all her children be killed within moments of their birth. On the night of Krishna's birth, a great glowing light lit up the kingdom of Mathura. The light was so bright it woke King Kamsa from his sleep. The light also brought a twist of fate with its shine. Vasudeva, the husband of Devaki, could not bear to see yet another one of his children murdered at the hands of the evil Kamsa. His intuition told him to escape the prison with the blue-black child and so he devised a plan.

When Vasudeva tried the prison door, to his surprise he found that it had been left open by a negligent guard. Like a sly fox, Vasudeva slipped through the prison gates and out into the city with Krishna bundled like a freshly baked loaf of bread in his arms. He took to the river Yamuna and sailed to a nearby cowherd community, where his dear friend Nanda and wife Yashoda lived. The loving couple had just given birth to a little girl that same night and Vasudeva pleaded that they swap the newborns so that Kamsa would not notice Devaki's child was missing. If he realised that her newborn was gone, he would command that every newborn child in the land be killed and so this was the only way to stop such evil doings. Nanda and Yashoda agreed and so they became the foster parents of Krishna.

Krishna grew up peacefully and dearly loved by all in the cowherd village. His rain cloud complexion and milky way eyes charmed all those who laid eyes upon him. Although he was a mischievous child and an unpleasant prankster, the victims of his vibrant childish play soon forgave the wide-eyed cherub. Yes, Krishna was a gracious gift to all in the cow village. The parents loved his playfulness and viewed him as their own. The boisterous boys would participate in Krishna's tricks, stealing freshly churned butter from hanging baskets and stuffing themselves full with big smiles on their faces. The wives and daughters could not resist his elegant flute playing and would come frolicking out of their homes to dance under the moonlight with Krishna, anytime they heard his sweet melodies. The love which followed Krishna was that of God's love in human childhood form. This purity of love was something which had not been experienced by the people before. Even the devas were stunned by the impact Krishna had over his loyal kinsmen.

One day, the charm of Krishna caught the attention of Lord Brahma, the god of material creation. Having seen the young Krishna slay a python ten times his size, Lord Brahma became bewildered by the boy's supreme abilities. What caught Brahma's attention the most was the way the ordinary cow herder was adored by his devotees as if he was Lord Vishnu himself. Being in disbelief that this small child could be greater than the ultimate supreme god, Lord Brahma decided to play a trick on Krishna to test his divinity. The divine creator of the material plane ventured down to earth and lingered out of sight in the flourishing forest. Krishna and his friends were joyfully playing while grazing their cows, blissfully unaware of the scheming Brahma.

While Krishna and his friends were occupied eating their meals, Lord Brahma abducted the grazing cows and placed them in the dreamland dimension from where he resides.

One of the boys who was watching the cows came rushing up the hill to where Krishna and his friends were enjoying their lunch, his face dripping in distress. The boy explained that all the cows had gone missing without even so much as a tail hair left behind to suggest their whereabouts. Krishna, being the valiant hero that he was, told the boy not to fret and reassured them that he would go to look for the cows while the rest of the boys continued to enjoy their midday feast.

Lord Brahma, eagerly entertained watched as Krishna left his friends to look for the cows that were no longer in their dimension. When the coast was clear, Lord Brahma put the same spell that he had cast on the cows onto the oblivious boys and banished them also to the dreamland dimension. Krishna, unaware of Brahma's games, continued to look for the disappearing cows. Although he did not know that Brahma had come to his dimension, he could sense that something was not quite right.

Having spent several hours vainly looking for the cows and their calves, Krishna returned to the hill where he and his friends had been enjoying their meal only to find his friends too were missing. Krishna then knew that this deception was one of divine nature and that it would be pointless to continue to look for the missing boys and cows. He also knew that the parents of the village would be devastated to hear that their beloved sons would no longer be returning home. If they found out they were missing, they would spend the rest of their days mourning and searching for cherished darlings who no longer existed.

Unwilling to go back to the cowherd village to the sights and sounds of grieving hearts, Krishna decided to use his divine grace to give the parents of the village what their hearts truly desired. Willing all the power of his being, Krishna split himself multiple times until there were enough Krishnas to replace all who had gone missing. Having known intimately the hearts of each boy and each cow, Krishna made it so that each avatar was a replica of the one who had gone missing. Each individual had been replaced in such a manner that their behaviours and characteristics were indistinguishable from the originals now asleep in Brahma's dream world. The only difference was that each replica carried a certain heavenly light that reflected the divinity of Krishna.

By the time the last missing boy had been replaced, it was late and the parents had already begun to conduct searches for their beloved boys and cherished cows. As if the dawn had come early, Krishna and the boys appeared on the horizon, lighting up the village with the glowing light of hope and cheer. The parents embraced their loved ones with a warmth that they had never experienced before. Although in appearance their children were the ones they had given birth to, now each child shined with the aura and love of Krishna that had filled the hearts of the village for so many years.

For an entire year, there was an abundance of love and happiness radiating from every home in the village. Every home was filled with the playfulness and joy of Krishna. The parents had never been happier with their children and the butchers struggled to take the cows to slaughter for their love for them was as great as the love they had for Krishna. The gift Krishna had given to the cow herders resembled heaven on earth. The bliss that overwhelmed the village travelled throughout the country and the divinity of Krishna grew in popularity as more and more devotees became attracted to the news of the Eden community.

Back in Brahma's world, the banished boys and cows were soundly sleeping and innocently ignorant of the magical merry land manifested in their replacement. For context, in Brahma's dimension one day is equivalent to 4.32 billion earth years, so for a year to have passed in Krishna's world, it was only but a moment in Brahma's world. Brahma had just finished putting the last of the boys to lay down tranquilly in the dreamland before returning to earth to see how Krishna was getting on. To his surprise, not only had a year already passed on earth but there in the village, Krishna and his friends were dancing joyfully to the sound of his gleeful flute.

Perplexed by the perceived power of Krishna, Brahma rushed down to Krishna's side and confronted the superhuman child whose capabilities seemed to exceed his own. Brahma, still in disbelief, demanded that Krishna reveal how he had performed these tricks. Krishna, brazen-faced, stopped playing his flute and smiled at Brahma. The skies suddenly filled with fluorescent green and violet light, which illuminated all that could be seen with the eye. Brahma looked around only to see thousands upon millions of Brahma all around him. Some were of similar likeness to the original Brahma with three heads, others had hundreds of heads but undoubtedly they were all he.

Bemused by the divinity of Krishna, Brahma immediately bowed down to the little blue boy, for he knew then in his

128

heart that Krishna was truthfully the complete incarnation of the supreme god. As Brahma grovelled at Krishna's feet, Krishna explained to Brahma that there exists more than just one universe. There were multiverses and all the Brahma's which surrounded them were summoned from the universes in which they ruled. At that moment, Brahma realised that he was only the creator of this universe and he thanked Krishna for giving him the gift of self-realisation.

Brahma, humbled by the infinite intelligence of Krishna, asked yet another question to clarify his misunderstandings. Brahma, using his mind's wisdom, could see the boys and cows who he had hidden safely asleep in the dreamland. What he didn't understand was how the same boys and cows were simultaneously standing before them on earth yet tucked away peacefully in his dimension. Krishna simply smiled valiantly and stared deep into Brahma's exhilarated eyes. In that instant, it was revealed to Brahma that all the boys and the cows were in reality extensions of Lord Vishnu the supreme god. This is when Brahma came to realise that the divinity of the supreme lived within all creations.

Brahma thanked Krishna for his mercy and asked him for forgiveness. Krishna gracefully forgave Brahma and asked that the boys and their cows be returned to earth. Brahma at once retrieved the sleeping captives and returned them to their proper place. Krishna then used his divine abilities to send all the Brahmas back to their original universes. He also dissolved all the avatars that he had made back into his body and with that harmony was restored.

Krishna's divinity is still celebrated by millions all over the globe who believe that he was the complete incarnation of the supreme Lord Vishnu. There are many tales and lessons to be learnt from this celebrated being but in the context of this chapter, what we have embarked upon should be understood like this: We were all created from the divine. Each individual cell in our body contains the infinite intelligence that some call God and others call the universe. If we can accept this concept, it is then true to say that we are all but incarnations of the divine one. We all possess the consciousness of the divine however we are in somewhat of a sleep state which keeps us ignorant of our true power. To live in a reality which meets our most superfluous expectations, we must journey to become one with the divine intelligence that slumbers blissfully within our subconscious. We must bring ourselves back home to the centre of our being so that we may find the truth of our creation, for there lies the power of ultimate manifestation.

9 ATTITUDE OF GRATITUDE

Gratitude is the ultimate state of receiving. It is the energetic and emotional condition of a desire achieved. When we are in a state of gratitude, our mind and body are working together harmoniously to embody our greatest manifestation. By using the law of cause and effect (which is detailed in the following chapter) we can bring our desired manifestation closer to us, by learning to remain in an attitude of gratitude.

Do you remember the last time you truly felt grateful for something and how great of a feeling it was? Try to remember now. Perhaps you thought you had lost your wallet when suddenly a stranger tapped you on the shoulder and said "you dropped this", returning all your money to you safely. Maybe you came home from a long, challenging day at work only to find that your partner cleaned the house, cooked you a lovely meal and the kids were soundly sleeping.

Perhaps you received a letter from your doctor telling you that the disease that had been causing you discomfort for so long has finally cleared up and would not be returning to your body.

The satisfaction of receiving something that relieves tension in your heart, the orgasmic feeling of merciful thankfulness has a potent power. The power of thankfulness sends signals from your mind into your body telling it that you have become what it is that you desired most. At that moment you have become one with your desired manifestation. Gratitude is such a powerful state of being because it uses both the mind and the body simultaneously to transform our state of being into one where we personify the desired outcome. When you are truly grateful, there is no doubt in the mind that you have realised your manifestation. With this definite realisation, you can stand firmly in your self knowing that you are who you say you are. When a state of gratitude is reached, feelings such as relaxation, exuberance, love and joy are felt within each cell of the body. For gratitude to work, the mind and the body must be in cohesion with one another so that the state may be truly satisfied.

Let us recognise here that there are different levels and intensities of gratitude that you can experience. Someone saving your loved one from drowning will be felt more intensely than someone paying for your car park fees. The reason we experience different intensities of gratitude is due to the level of desire we have for the attainment of an object at any given moment. Gratitude is measured by what is felt most prominently in the heart. When we are using an attitude of gratitude as a manifestation technique, we want to be aiming for the deepest level of gratitude that we can achieve. When we feel a great sense of gratitude, something within us automatically wishes to 'return the favour'. This feeling of reciprocity motivates us to take the necessary action which will bring about more of what we felt grateful for. Through this action, we can coordinate the components which will realise our deepest desires.

An attitude of gratitude, when felt in the body, inspires the mind to focus on the things which brought that state into being. The subconscious mind then marries these bodily feelings with physical activities that will motivate us to do these actions again so that we can be gratified once more. This aspect of gratitude is truly amazing. By its very nature, gratitude aligns the mind and body into a state of oneness. Gratitude is one of the only emotions within the human capacity which aligns us with the pure state of oneness effortlessly and free of conflicting emotions.

You cannot be truly grateful and dissatisfied at the same time. Gratitude is one of the most divine realities that we as humans can clothe ourselves in. Along with unconditional love, gratitude is a state of being which is an extension of God or the All Consciousness that we have termed it previously. When we tap into our abilities to be grateful, we are directly communicating and becoming a facet of the divine creative intelligence living within us.

So how can we begin to practice a genuine attitude of gratitude to aid us with our manifestations? The easiest way you can start is by being grateful for all the things you already have all around you, whether big or small. Before you wake up every new day and before you lay down to go to sleep, you can count fifty things in your life that you are grateful for. You may be grateful for the warm home you live in or for having running water and food to eat. You may be thankful for the rain that waters your garden and the air which fills your lungs. You may be thankful to be a parent, or you may express gratitude that you have a source of income. You may be thankful for a mentor or for an individual that makes you smile. Maybe you are thankful for a community that you have found or for the support you have gained in aiding you with a project. You may be thankful for knowing what your talents are and that you have the tools and opportunity to pursue them. Maybe you are thankful for the sun that brightens up your day or the stars which enchant the night sky. You can even give thanks for having a body that allows you to be physically active or for ears that allow you to hear melodic music.

When you intentionally stop everything you are doing and focus exclusively on being thankful for the things which you already have, you realise that there are countless things for which to be thankful; things that you already possess. Look around and see that you are abundant with things that make your life bright and easy. Counting all your blessings daily is a great devotional practice that will tune your being into an attitude of gratitude. By doing this routine regularly it will eventually become a habit and the world around you will become angelic.

At first, you may find it difficult to point out fifty things that you are truly grateful for and so you may want to acquire some tools that can help you. The first tool I will mention is prayer beards. You can purchase or even make a necklace or bracelet that is made up of fifty beads. You can then hold these beads in your hand and starting from one end, count the things that you are grateful for by threading an individual bead through your fingertips each time that you find something to be grateful for. By the time you reach the end of the chain, you would have found fifty things to be grateful for. The more you do this the faster and the better you will become.

Another tool that you can use is scripting or in layman's terms, getting a pen and paper and writing down fifty things that you are grateful for. This may seem like a laborious task but actually, once you get started you will realise that you can complete the task within 20 minutes. Again the more that you do it, the more efficient you will become at finding things to be grateful for. On your page, number your lines 1-50 and list all that you are grateful for that day, this will help you keep track of your list.

The last tool that I will mention that you can use to help tune your being into an attitude of gratitude is by laying down or sitting in a quiet room, preferably with your eyes closed, while listening to a guided gratitude meditation on youtube, or whatever digital source is your preference. These guided meditations list hundreds of things to be grateful for and you can easily focus your attention on the words while letting the tones and intentions be absorbed by your being. If you can not find a youtube video which you prefer to help you with this, then you can use the one I have uploaded here:

https://youtu.be/ZYF8PtBY-zM

Getting into an attitude of gratitude, especially if you are quite a pessimistic person, is not a one-off task. You must practice finding things to be grateful for every single day for a minimum of twenty-one days and beyond. If you can have this practice for twenty-one days, you will find that your subconscious mind begins to be programmed into the attitude of gratitude and naturally you will begin to drift into the god consciousness where oneness and grace become you.

It is the grace that comes from the attitude of gratitude that magnetises your desired manifestations to you. When grace emulates from your being, more people, places and things in which you can find gratitude start to find you, without you being consciously aware or active in their manifestation. You will be a walking orb of harmony and happiness because you have become, in essence, likened to the divine.

If we want to use our attitude of gratitude to bring about the things which are not yet physically seen in our 3D reality, we can start using the simple practice of visualisation within our mind's eye. As I mentioned before, the state of gratitude relates to the mind and the body being harmonious with the supreme force. The supreme force is the source of all things and therefore is responsible for the creation of all things which we are to be grateful for. Due to this law, if we can tune our body and our mind to be grateful for the things which we do not already have, we can convey the message to the supreme force that we are imminently receiving the things that we visualised being grateful for.

In a quiet room, preferably with your eyes closed, picture in your mind a scene with you directly in it. Fill the scene with the thing that you desire most. If it is a new home, picture yourself in that home walking around the rooms with the keys in your hand and the deed on the table. Walk over to the table and see your name printed in black ink, stating that you are the owner of that home. Now pay attention to your heart. How does it feel to own that home? Fill your heart with excitement and feel the joy light up a smile on your face. Now say thank you as many times as you desire. Feel the relief and satisfaction of owning that home as it illuminates your entire being. Thank the supreme force which has granted you the ability to visualise your dream and give thanks knowing that the simple visualisation within the attitude of gratitude is sending a wave of fortune in your direction. While you are in this visualisation, move around the scene and go into as much detail as you possibly can. See the things which you desire and every time you feel your heart get excited while joy floods your body, say thank you and express gratitude in the most intense form of satisfaction that you possibly can.

Beyond visualisation, we can manifest our desires using the attitude of gratitude by actually going and physically touching the things that we desire. If it is a brand new sports car that you desire the most, why not go to the nearest car garage that houses the car you desire and book a test drive. Put on the clothes that you see yourself wearing when you will finally own the car. Spray yourself with the perfume that will fragrance the car once you own it. When you arrive at the garage go all out! Get into the car, hold the keys and feel the material that makes the car. Focus on that physical feeling and in your mind, speak to yourself as if it is already yours. Tell yourself how much you love owning this car and express how grateful you are to have it in your possession. Let the satisfaction of finally being inside this car fill your being. Convey gratitude to the supreme source of all desires and manifestations for allowing you to have your dream car. Smile and let joy overwhelm your being.

Visualisation is a key tool in manifesting when in the attitude of gratitude as it allows your mind to perceive the wish as coming to pass. So if you have the chance, take a picture of yourself in the car, the clothes or the dream home and put that picture somewhere where you can visualise it regularly. If you are not able to go and physically touch and take pictures with the thing which you are to be grateful for, then go onto the internet and get images of the thing you desire. If you can, create a vision board and print this out so that you can put it somewhere in your home or your office where your eyes can look at your dreams frequently. If you can not print them out, then make the mood board or image your screensaver. This will allow you to lay your eyes upon them daily.

Every time you see the image of all the dreams and pending manifestations that you have, thank the supreme god force which holds your desires in the infinite source of everything and let the attitude of gratitude take over you. Even without having the things that you truly desire right now in your physical presence, you can still express a subtle state of gratitude simply by feeling thankful that your wishes are on their way to you. It is this simple technique, this tiny shift in your paradigm that will create a tremendous wave of fortune and favour in your direction. Practice gratitude daily and become the witness and testimony of God's saving grace.

In the beginning of time, even before the concept of time, the supreme god Ra emerged from the primordial waters of Nun, dripping in darkness. At this time Ra was known as Atum, for he resembled the nothingness of the night sky.

Using the sacred powers that lay within his mystical name, Ra called upon the magical forces of Heka as well as the wisdom of Tehuti and created the sun in the dawning sky. As light took its place in the universe through his ultimate powers, Ra began to call upon the mysterious forces and gave name to the earth, Geb, and then to the sky, Nut. He also named the winds, Shu and the rain, Tefnut. Ra gave every star in every constellation a name as well as every blade of grass and every fruit tree. He breathed life into the goddess of the river and gods of the natural plan, so that they may govern over everything he had created in perfect harmony.

With that, the world had been created however Ra was not yet satisfied. To quench his thirst for creativity, he created mankind and eventually took on the form of man so that he could govern over them as the first Pharaoh. Thanks to Ra, all was in perfect balance and humanity lived harmoniously on earth. They lived in perfect equilibrium for many generations and sure enough, Ra in his human form began to grow old and grey.

After a while, the subjects of Ra began to question his ability to properly rule the new age of humanity that had come into being. They questioned whether his ancient wisdom was truly in touch with the needs of the current generation on earth and jeered at his silver wiry hair. Upon listening in on the private conversations of his subjects, Ra soon came to realise that humanity was plotting against him. He was astonished to find out that despite all the beauty he had created on earth, his subjects were trying to figure out ways that they could overthrow him and relinquish his powers.

Ra grew angry over the ungrateful attitudes he heard humanity expressing, for how could they forget that it was he who was responsible for the rivers they drank from, the seeds which they ate and the sun which they frequently basked in. What angered Ra the most however was how disobedient humanity was to the natural laws which created harmony on earth. Ra created the world in such a beautiful manner that there was no need for sin and suffering; however, the ingratitude of humanity was beginning to disrupt the perfect paradise he had created.

Ra had finally had enough of the ungrateful ways of humanity and decided to retreat from the earth and consult his council in heaven. Ra summoned Shu, Tefnut, Geb, Nut as well as Nun, the father and mother of his creation. When all the gods and goddesses came beside him, they bowed down so that their foreheads touched the ground where his feet were placed. Nun spoke and said "My son, why have you called us here today". Ra explained what he had seen and heard on earth and told his council of the plots mankind had made against him. He told them of the sins, which came from ingratitude, which were giving birth to imperfections on earth. Ra told them that although he was angry at humanity, he could not bring himself to slay mankind and so sought the advice of the council as to what he should do with his ungrateful creation.

Down on earth, the absence of the great gods who governed over the natural laws was already causing chaos and the council watched as humanity raced around in a flurry of sin. It was evident that the power of Ra was honourable and mighty. If he were to personally set wrath on humanity, he would completely obliterate them in an instant. With this observation, the council agreed that it would be best for Ra to stay comfortably seated on his throne and instead send his 'eye' to do his bidding in the form of the lioness goddess Hathor-Sekhmet. Ra agreed and gave life to his daughter Hathor-Sekhmet by speaking her name.

Hathor-Sekhmet Descended from heaven to earth and began to carry out Ra's commands. And she painfully punished humanity. Each day she would seek out humans to slay. Young, old, male, female to the blood-thirsty Hathor-Sekhmet it did not matter. As soon as she had set her vengeful eyes on the victim, innocent of sin or not, she would prey upon them, covering her mane in fresh flesh and brand new blood. Hathor-Sekhmet went on this way for many days, slaying any person she came across. With each new taste of blood, Hathor-Sekhmet's blood-lust grew stronger and stronger until the point that no one kill could satisfy her.

Ra, seated upon his throne, watched his daughter Hathor-Sekhmet wreck havoc on humanity and soon began to repent. He knew that if she carried on this way, within no time there would be no one left to slain! Ra called his

daughter back to the heavens but it was too late.
Hathor-Sekhmet had worked herself up into a blood-lust
frenzy that she could not hear the commands of her father.
Her heart was filled with joy each time she slew a man and
the smell of blood ruled her. Ra knew that he would not be
able to stop Hathor-Sekhmet unless he used his wisdom to
cun her out of her slaughterous-hypnotic state.

Ra ordered for seven thousand pails of beer, mixed with red
ochre, to be released into the pools which homed her sacred
dwelling place in Dendra. After one particularly eventful
evening of barbarous blood-shed, Hathor-Sekhmet returned
to her sacred site and fell asleep under the moonlight;
recharging before resuming her merciless creed. While she
slept, Ra flooded the pools around her with the seven
thousand pails of bright red beer, which resembled human
blood as it glistened in the light of the heavenly bodies above.

When Hathor-Sekhmet awoke, she saw that her paws were
covered in the synthetic pseudo and began to lick them.
Enjoying the sweetness of the fresh 'blood' Ra had laid out
for her, she began slurping up the beer until she became fully
intoxicated and soon passed out. Hathor-Sekhmet remained
inebriated in her sleep for some time, while the setting sun
and the rising moon watched her slumber.

The next day, Hathor-Sekhmet rose from where she had
passed out feeling refreshed and as bright as a daisy.
Hathor-Sekhmet rejoiced by the light of the new day and
laughed uncontrollably as love and desire filled her heart. As
the rays of the dawn touched her skin, Hathor-Sekhmet's
mane fell off and her lioness head was transformed into that

of a cow's. With that, Hathor-Sekhmet became Hathor, the gentle mother goddess who with her transformation brought peace to humanity. All of mankind rejoiced at the presence of Hathor and gave undying gratitude to her transformation. It was with her transformation that harmony was restored to the earth once again. All the people's hearts shone with glee and they threw festivals and lavish banquets for consecutive days where they drank beer and filled their hearts with joy, grace and gratitude. With this, the worship of Hathor became a tradition in which the people to whom she had shown mercy would look to their left hand daily and find five things to be grateful for.

The five gifts of Hathor are a reminder to her followers and the reader that daily gratitude is a necessary practice to live a life full of light, hope and desired manifestations. In this ancient Kemet creation story, it was the people's ingratitude which brought turmoil and hardship into their life. Sometimes we get caught up with wanting more out of life and stricken by desire that we forget to be thankful for what we already have in life.

Gratitude, and the joy it brings, is an emotion of the highest order. It is a mystical force which relates directly to the heart of the creator. It bothered Ra that the people were expressing ingratitude because their ungratefulness gave birth to sin and imbalance in the human and heavenly world. There is a magical power behind the emotion of gratitude and just by finding five things to be grateful for each day, you can move out of darkness and into a state of transformation and light. The representation of beer in the story of Hathor's transformation is also of great significance. It illustrates the feeling one is to feel when in a state of gratitude. It is one of pure joy and release of inhibitions. There is no space for worry or feelings of suffering when one is intoxicated with the feeling of gratitude. One becomes completely exhilarated and free. It is a taste of bliss that anyone can take the time to feel just by finding a handful of things to be grateful for each day and meditating upon them. Embrace the feeling of gratitude by inviting joy into your heart and watch the effortless transformation of your life.

10 THE LAW OF CAUSE AND EFFECT

For every cause in the entire scope of the universe there is a corresponding effect. This is the fundamental law that exists throughout our universe. Everything that has ever occurred or has ever come into existence, has come to be because of a series of events that first took place. Nothing in our universe comes to be through randomisation, everything can be linked back to a chain of events which made it so. Consciously knowing this, we can easily predict what the future outcome for a person or situation will be. For example, we can predict that if a person eats only plant-based foods and does thousands of sit-ups for a year, they are going to have significantly firmer abs than the person who does zero exercise for the year and eats sugary, gluten-based foods. It was of no coincidence that the person who ate well and worked out every day obtained a physique greater in aesthetics than the person who ate poorly and did nothing.

The cause of the aesthetic physique was consistent healthy eating and exercise.

This observation can be made for practically everything within our human understanding. There is no such thing as fate. All things can be traced back to a sure enough, succession of causes that brought about their effects. Nothing simply comes out of the oblivion. Things may occur that you are oblivious to because you have not been aware of their causes, but they did not come randomly out of nothingness. All things come from the all, the one rhythmic song that contains within it a divine order. When we have a full understanding of this harmonious chain of cause and effect, we can better control the conditions of our world.

A relatable phenomenon that gives light to your awareness of cause and effect, is that sudden and mystical moment of clarity you experience with déjà vu. If you have ever experienced déjà vu, you know that for just a moment your entire reality seems to warp around you and seemingly you have an instinctive feeling that you have already seen the scene playing out in front of you. Déjà Vu is like watching a three-second replay of your life, although from your place of awareness it was the first time you experienced being in that scene.

The peculiar perception of déjà vu is only our observation or awareness of an effect which has followed a succession of causes. When we experience déjà vu, for that moment our subconscious mind is harmoniously synchronised with our conscious mind to the point where we have now become aware of all the causes leading up to that moment. For that moment, we are so aware of the law of cause and effect that we can predict in our conscious mind exactly what will happen in the scene playing out before us. If you have experienced déjà vu, you know that it is possible to predict the precise outcome of an effect; right down to the colour of a car, the words of a co-worker or the formation of the clouds above. In moments of déjà vu, we experience the mind of the All Consciousness, which lives under a veil within our subconscious mind. In case you need reminding, this is the mind which knows all, sees all and experiences all as already complete.

So how can we use sensations like déjà vu and our current understanding of cause and effect to adequately predict and become the effect which we want to see in our lives? Well, we must first grasp and understand this observable truth as law. Consciousness is the cause of everything and all manifestations are an effect of consciousness. Your state of being, along with the thoughts and images that you create in your mind, are the centre of causation for everything that manifests into your reality. Everything that has manifested into your physical world is a result of who you believe yourself to be within consciousness. Firstly, within your consciousness, you have the belief and the thought about what your reality should look like; this is the cause. Following these thoughts in consciousness, you confirm your belief by interacting with the physical world in a way that reflects your beliefs; these are the effects. At every moment, we are creating the world that we wish to see through consciousness. Through interaction with our physical world, we confirm what we believe ourselves to be, as an effect of consciousness.

When we think about the mechanics of cause and effect, we can think of it existing on a scale. To do this, visualise a see-saw where one side represents your desired state and the other its absolute opposite/undesired state. The pivot of the see-saw is your consciousness and the position of the see-saw is your observation of what has manifested. When you experience yourself as 'up' on the see-saw, you are in the effect of who you truly believe yourself to be. You will know when you are aligned with who you believe yourself to be because you will experience positive emotions. In this moment of being up on the see-saw you have become the desired effect that your consciousness wishes to observe. When you are up on the see-saw, living the effect that you wish to see, simultaneously there is a version of yourself which is down and represents the opposite of your desired reality. Just by shifting consciousness (the cause) on the pivot of the see-saw, you can lift the other side of the see-saw up and observe it as an effect. If you begin to feel negative feelings it is because through consciousness, you have given cause to an effect which does not reflect who you truly believe yourself to be. At the same time that our consciousness observes that we are not in the state we wish to be in, it also observes the desired state which is on the opposite side of the spectrum or in terms of our analogy, at the opposite side of the see-saw. We can obtain the desired state simply by shifting our consciousness to the opposite side of the see-saw and use it to lift the effect of who we believe ourselves to be.

The concept of cause and effect is one of the more challenging concepts to grasp in this book. Many masters of mind and manifestation have studied this phenomenon and gone through the laborious task of re-programming their minds so that they can make use of what is being said here. Since it is somewhat of a challenge to grasp the concept I will put it another way for your understanding. First thing is first, your consciousness (what you give your attention to) is the cause of everything that you can perceive in this world. It is the father in conception. Your feelings (your desires for what you wish to see and be) are the way that you, as your human self, communicate with your consciousness (your consciousness is directly linked to the All Consciousness/ God the father.) Your feelings and desires, therefore, are the mother in conception. When your consciousness, that which gives you awareness of being or the father, is married to your feelings and desires or the mother, an effect is conceived in the womb of the physical 3D plane. You then experience the effect of this conception on the physical plane through its manifestation. You are therefore the son; the one who can perceive consciously and feel emotionally the manifestation which you can taste, touch, see, hear and smell. All matter that we can experience through the five senses is born in this way. First consciousness (the cause/the father) marries a desire (the mother) which is felt through our human emotion.

Once a desire is consciously perceived we will manifest it by incubating it in our human imagination, therefore, giving it divine attention. When we think about the joy that having something will bring us, our conscious mind begins to perceive that which we desire to see in the physical plane which gives birth to an effect. In the same breath, we can also manifest the things which we do not wish to see. When we focus our attention on those things which give us bad feelings consciously or unconsciously, we create a cause in our imagination. By picturing in our mind's eye scenarios that place us somewhere we would rather not live, we will it to manifest by feeling the emotions associated with it.

The consciousness of the All, (the father/the cause) communicates with us through our feelings. What is important to note is that the All Consciousness does not understand the duality of emotions but deals in polarity. It also does not understand the concept of positive or negative emotions. For the All Consciousness, everything is a desire to bring about an effect. Happy and sad to the All Consciousness is one of the same thing, only they live on opposite sides of the spectrum. For example: if you feel terribly sad about something, the All Consciousness understands this as a desire to also feel happiness. To the All Consciousness, when you perceive yourself as not being that which you desire to be, on the same spectrum you are that which you desire to be only you are experiencing it in another light.

As an example, let's say that you lost a loved one and are feeling depressed because you perceive in consciousness that you will no longer have any memories of this person or that you have an empty place in your heart for them. You perceive this to be true because you give attention to their absence as well as feeling emotions of loss and grief. You have given a cause to the effect. However, if you were to perceive the loss in another light, a different effect would be born. The fact that you perceive you will no longer have memories with this person is because you have already made many memories with them. These memories live in your consciousness and are readily retrievable anytime you decide to give your attention to them. The fact that you may perceive an empty place in your heart for the deceased loved one is because there is already a place that exists in your heart where they belong. The manifestation of grief and absence, the effect, only exists because you perceive these feelings to be true. In consciousness, when you observe the opposite side of the spectrum to be true, you will experience the effect of bliss and the eternal presence of your deceased loved one so that they live within your desired state forevermore.

The same can be true when we feel frustration or impatience when we are manifesting abundance. If we consciously perceive lack all around us, then this is what we are telling the All Consciousness that we are. By focusing our attention on lack and giving it a feeling on the emotional spectrum, we are creating more lack in our physical reality. However, if we pay attention to the abundance which is already around us, we are telling the All Consciousness that we believe ourselves to be the abundant effect we desire and therefore will create more physical abundance for us in the material realm. Whether you feel happy about your perceived poverty or sadness, you are still giving your attention to it and when married with emotion, will manifest it.

Consciousness is who we believe ourselves to be. All that we see around us in physical manifestation is a representation of consciousness confirming who we believe ourselves to be. We are the cause of everything that we see in our reality. Whether we like this idea or not, this is a truth which once grasped can set us free.

So what techniques can we begin to use so that we can become the effect which we wish to see? The easiest way for us to begin to intercept causes which come from our past programming, and are responsible for the effects we see today, is to impress upon our conscious mind the images and feelings of having already obtained the desired manifestation, now in the present moment. We can use the powers which reside in the mind's eye, along with our human emotion to warp space around us so that we evidently become the person who possesses the desired manifestation. You can do this right now. For example: in the room that you are in, think of an object that you wish to possess that is not currently in the room with you. Close your eyes and in the space which you wish the desired object to occupy, remove all objects and things which are currently occupying the space. Now that the space is empty, fill it with the object that you most desire. Now capture the feeling of actually having this object there in the room with you. Feel the excitement and anticipation of being able to immediately reach out and touch it. Feel that you can get up from where you are seated right now and interact with it at will. In this exercise, you have controlled matter through your mind's eye and not your physical eyes. You have successfully become the effect that you wish to be and see. Due to the law of cause and effect, you have now set into motion the causes which will take place to make this effect appear in your physical reality.

We can take this one step further. Still with the object in the same room as you and the feeling that it is there before you, picture yourself reminiscing about how the object came to you. Maybe it came to you through a delivery or was gifted to you by a loved one. By reminiscing about how the object came to you, you have successfully impressed upon consciousness the exact sequence of events that came before the desired effect. When you become the leading effect by using the same technique of imagining and feeling, you have also become the cause of the desired effect.

To summarise, the fundamentals of the law of cause and effect is that: there can be no effect without its subsequent cause. Everything that came into the physical plane came to be because something was the cause of its manifestation. The two concepts of cause and effect are intimately interlinked and it is impossible to have one without inducing the other. When considering cause and effect for manifestation, we realise that when we understand this principle in detail, we can have sovereignty over the effects that we see in our physical reality. All effects, all physical manifestations that come in our 3D existence, are all a result of causation within consciousness.

Although you are a powerful manifester, you can not always be in control of the exact causation of events that will take place leading up to an effect. Life is a complex symphony and the divine order of things come from a place far beyond our human comprehension. Although this is true, one thing that we can have control of in this marriage between consciousness and emotions is the energetic appearance of the effect. Through our human emotions and imagery within our mind's eye, we can become the effect of that which we wish to be in an instant. We do not have to wait for a long line of causation that may or may not happen because of past causations and effects. We can take control of our material world at this moment simply by feeling as if we have already become the person who possesses the desired manifestation.

To understand this law we must first understand this. Consciousness is the cause and manifestation is the effect. This is the principle behind the law of cause and effect and must always be remembered. Once we begin practising becoming the cause within consciousness, the new person who we perceive ourselves to be will emerge. For example: if before you go to bed, you picture and feel like you acquired something luxurious, the next day when you have come out of the practice you will find yourself thinking with a more liberal attitude to money. You may also find yourself desiring more luxurious experiences or items as you have now become the person who complements the cause of acquiring such items. The more we stay in the practice, the stronger and more harmonious our manifestations will become.

To become a master manifester, you must perceive yourself as the person who naturally experiences the desires you want to see. If your current environment does not necessarily reflect the exact effects you wish to see, you must begin to see your environment gradually morphing into the desired manifestation. You must see yourself as becoming that which you want to manifest, as opposed to seeing yourself as lacking what you desire. The marrying of consciousness and emotions produces who we perceive ourselves to be when we say I am. It is through the statement 'I am' and what follows after it that gives us a reflection of what is currently being perceived in consciousness. Our feelings give us guidance as to whether this perception of self is correctly aligned with our truest desires. The objects, places and people we interact with daily confirm who we believed ourselves to be previous to its manifestation.

This is the holy trinity of creation: the all-knowing consciousness (the father), the desired feeling or emotional state in which thoughts are incubated (the mother) and finally your experience of self and the extended manifestations with which you interact daily (the son.) Once you have mastered the law of cause and effect, the world is your playground.

The biblical story of Isaac beautifully illustrates how we can use our knowledge of cause and effect practically to become the master of all our manifestations. In 1836 BC, Rebekah wife of Isaac, gave birth to a set of twins named Esau and Jacob. Esau was the firstborn of the twins and he arrived into the world a bright crimson, covered from head to toe in a suit of hair. Holding onto his heel Jacob, the smooth-skinned, second twin came following in close behind his hairy brother.

Before her sons were born, Rebekah received a prophecy that the two would become opposing nations, with one far greater in strength than the other. As the prophecy predicted, the two brothers grew up with different interests and different destinies. Because their interests were so dissimilar, their parents found a favourite between them. Esau was a skilful hunter and loved venturing in the wild among the beasts. Esau would seek out rare and exotic animals, often for weeks at a time before returning home with his kill. Isaac, their father, also loved hunting and eating game stew so naturally favoured Esau of the two twins. Jacob, on the other hand, liked to stay at home with the women and so was highly favoured by his mother. He would keep Rebekah company at the tents while they cooked delightful food and shared colourful stories which filled her days with joy.

On one particular day, Esau had been away from the tents for many days without any successful hunts. He returned to their home frail and famished only to find his younger brother Jacob cooking up a beautifully tasty stew, which was fragrant with spices. Desperate and craving, Esau begged his brother for some of the irresistible stew that was bubbling away on the stove. Jacob agreed that he would give his starving brother some of the food but on one condition: Esau must willingly give up his birthright and assign it over to Jacob. Esau, starving and anguished from his hunger, agreed that he would trade his birthright over to Jacob. Jacob made Esau swear an oath that Esau's birthright now belonged to him. The famished Esau sealed the oath by tucking into the stew his brother had prepared with bread and wine, satisfied with his decision.

Some years passed and Esau married while their father, Isaac, grew old and weary. Having spent many days of his life out in the blinding sun, Isaac's eyesight had diminished. In his wiser years, he relied solely on touch and his other senses to identify the world around him. Isaac knew that his days were limited and so wanted to be sure that he gave his eldest son the blessing that was his by right of birth. Isaac invited his son Esau to his quarters and told him that he was ready to give him his birthright blessing. This blessing would honour the firstborn with an abundance of wealth and descendants for generations to come. Isaac promised to give this blessing to Esau but requested that first he go out into the open country to hunt some game and prepare it in the way that he enjoyed most. Isaac promised Esau that upon his return from the successful hunt, he would be willing to give him his blessing.

Rebekah, who was not far from the conversation, heard her husband's promise to their eldest son. Although Rebekah loved Esau, she did not approve of the women whom he had married and favoured her youngest son Jacob. When she was sure that Esau had gone with his bow and arrow to hunt the game that Isaac had requested, she went to Jacob and told him what she had heard. She told her son that she wished for him to have his father's blessing and so devised a ploy to get Isaac to bless Jacob in the place of Esau. She told Jacob to go to his father's field and kill two goat calves so that she may prepare the tender meat, just the way that Isaac liked. She then told Jacob, that once the food was prepared, he was to go to his father and present the food to him, so that he would give the blessing to the youngest son.

 Jacob agreed to his mother's plot but protested that his father would be able to tell that he was not Esau. He feared that if Isaac found out about the deception, Isaac would surely curse him instead of blessing him. How would he be able to deceive his father when his brother Esau was covered in hair yet he was a smooth-skinned man. Rebekah told Jacob not to worry and to go to the field for the goat calves as she had told him. When Jacob returned, Rebekah skinned the goats and prepared some food just the way her husband loved. She then used the skins of the goat calves and placed them on the arms and neck of Jacob, so that he felt as hairy as his older brother. She then took some clothes of Esau, which smelled of him and put them on her beloved son

Jacob. With her son and the food prepared, Rebekah sent Jacob to his father's tent so that he may receive the birthright blessing.

With the plot prepared, Jacob went to the tent where his father was resting and announced himself as Esau. He told his blind father that he had returned from the hunt with tasty food and was ready to receive his blessing. Isaac, still wise in his old age, asked the disguised Jacob how he had returned from the open country so quickly. Jacob replied that his success had come from the Lord. Isaac was doubtful of his answer and asked the imposter to come close to him so that he could feel if it were truly Esau.

Jacob approached Isaac and Isaac reached out to touch his son's arms. Isaac felt the hairy arms of Jacob and was convinced in himself that they were the arms of Esau, even though the voice that owned the arms was that of his younger son Jacob. He asked Jacob if he was indeed Esau and Jacob replied that he was. Somewhat convinced that the person before him was truly his eldest son, Isaac told the undercover Jacob to bring the food so that he may enjoy the offering before giving him the blessing that he had promised.

Jacob presented the food to Isaac and Isaac ate to his heart's delight. Isaac then told Jacob to come to him once more so that he could kiss him. Jacob placed his cheek to his father's lips and as he did so, Isaac could smell the clothes that he wore which were covered in the fragrance of Esau. Relieved to smell his eldest son, Isaac was happy to give his blessing. Isaac blessed Jacob with an abundance of riches from the heavens and the earth. He made him a great nation of obedient servants and lord over his siblings. Isaac blessed Jacob with grain and wine and blessed all those who blessed him and cursed all those who cursed him. Once Isaac had finished giving Jacob the birthright blessing and was satisfied with the ceremony, his crafty son slipped out of the tent.

In anticipation to receive the blessing of his father, Esau returned home shortly after and began to prepare the game that he had successfully hunted. Once prepared, Esau went to the tent of his father and announced himself as the firstborn son, who had brought offerings to the father and was ready to receive his blessing. Isaac's heart sunk in his chest and he trembled with disbelief. He announced to his eldest son that the blessing had already been given to his youngest son Jacob, who just moments before had come in place of him with a deceptive disguise. Horrified by the news, Esau bawled and begged his father to also bless him. Empathetic to his son's cries, Isaac held his son but regretfully informed him that the birthright blessing had already been given to Jacob and so it would be Jacob who received the abundance he had decreed. Esau begged his father with tears of sorrow streaming down his distraught face but Isaac only had these words to comfort his son.

"Your dwelling will be away from the earth's richness, away from the dew of heaven above. You will live by the sword and you will serve your brother. But when you grow restless, you will throw his yoke from off your neck."

The story of Jacob and Esau symbolically demonstrates not only the nature of cause and effect but also the practices that may be used so that we may become the effect that we wish to see. In the early part of the story, when Esau came back famished from hunting, we see how you can be the cause of an effect even if it is not the effect you desire to become. When Esau gave over his birthright to Jacob for the sake of instant gratification he 'despised' his blessing to the birthright. Because he was so concerned with his current situation, he was willing to give up all the glory that was meant for him. Esau obliviously gave up his blessing from Isaac just so that he could appease his hunger at that moment. Instead of holding faith that he was to be blessed with plenty more, he commissioned an act that caused a sequence of events whereby the birthright blessing would be given to his brother, Jacob. It was his immediate discomfort, his observation of things in his immediate environment not being to his liking, which caused him to create an effect which took away his birthright blessing. If only he had been consciously aware of the cause he was creating, he could have prevented losing his birthright to his younger brother.

The act of Jacob's betrayal symbolically illustrates how we can use our senses and feelings to communicate to the All Consciousness that we are already the effect that we wish to see. It was the Mother, Rebekah, who first had the desire to manifest the birthright blessing onto her son Jacob. Jacob then becomes like the effect, by dressing as Esau and therefore replacing the existing manifestation with the desired manifestation. By dressing himself in the appearance of the firstborn, Jacob is embodying the effect that he wishes to see at that very moment. When Isaac touched and smelt the manifester, Jacob, he was sensorily convinced that Jacob was indeed Esau. In that moment, Jacob had communicated with the All Consciousness (the father), that he was the one who was rightfully to receive the blessing. It was through his conviction that the father made cause to the manifested effect, which was Jacob being blessed in place of Esau.

It is also important to take from this biblical story that Jacob remained close to the home of his father Isaac and was always by his mother Rebekah's side. Esau however would spend many weeks at a time away from his father's home. To give this interpretation: Jacob was frequently with the desire (the mother) and remained in the presence of All Consciousness (the father). For these reasons alone, Jacob became a master manifester. Esau on the other hand went frequently into the material world, the open country, to forcibly and laboriously hunt his success. By taking 'matters into his own hands' and without the help of his father and mother, Esau took away from the promise of abundance which was his birthright and inherited far less. Keep your father and mother married in harmonious union and watch the sons of your heaven be born onto you.

11 Surrendering/Devotion

Our fundamental limitation as manifesters living in the human condition is that we are limited by our belief systems. We came into this world with a magnificent mind and a capable body, equipped to create and manipulate energy. All things which we wish to see, taste, hear, touch and smell would be harmoniously available to us in just moments if we had the patience to align ourselves completely with divine order. Unfortunately, we are living in an age where within the human condition, we have fallen into a deep amnesiac sleep and forgotten fundamentally who we are. The powers of the omnipotent creator are available to each and every one of us however many of us are living in paradigms which do not support this truth. If you are seeking to become a master manifester, not just for one day but for every day, it is your duty to wake up to the full truth of who you are. You will need to commit yourself to the journey of self-mastery if you want to continually produce the outcomes of who and what you wish to be. To manifest seamlessly and with minimal conflict always and forever, you must become a master manifester.

The difficulty of achieving the status of master manifester comes through the belief system of the ego. For many, their egoic paradigm says that they are helpless humans whose lives and circumstances are destined to be the way that they are because of where they were born and who they were born to. Our parents, our class and our schooling have constructed in our minds a character within the ego that we have become so attached to that we believe this is truly who we are. Although as a human it is necessary to have an ego for self-identity (so that we know how to conduct ourselves daily without feeling disorientated) we do not need to become attached to the identity which we have created.

For the most part, what we believe about ourselves simply is not true. Many of the opinions we have about ourselves come from the projected thoughts and beliefs of other people. These outside voices that echo through our mind have absolutely nothing to do with the essence of who we truly are or the feeling we have about ourselves within our souls. Had you been born under another star, in another location and to different parents, you would have a completely different perspective of yourself and therefore you would live a completely different destiny to the one you have since created for yourself. If it is true that we come into existence unaware of ego or identity until we are given one by our parents and society, then it is also true that we can not fully trust the identity and ideas that we have about ourselves.

There have been many times in our life that we have been so sure that we wanted something that we would go so far as to sacrifice everything just so we would obtain it. We do all this only to realise a few months later that the thing we had once desired so much and did so much to obtain, now totally repulses us. If you are struggling to accept this concept, just think back to a time you had a lover or an ex that you desired so passionately. Now reflect on some of the emotions that you currently hold for them. For many people, they despise their ex-lover. In fact, one in two marriages in the west end in divorce. How can it be that fifty per cent of people who were once so certain that committing themselves to another would bring them the life they desired, ended up in a situation where they no longer desired this specific concept of marriage. How can they now despise the person/idea that they had once been so sure of?

Reflecting on this, how can we come to trust our own decisions and desires when so many times we have been betrayed by our own limited egoic beliefs. How are we to become masters of our destiny when for many of us we do not know what we want. Even when we think we know what we want, over time this belief is subject to change. As we journey through life unveiling more of who we are, we begin to learn more about what it is that we do want and what it is that we do not want. This is the journey all in life must go through. We are constantly moulding and refining the true nature of who we are by manifesting situations that serve us and make us happy. In contrast, we also manifest situations that do not serve us and make us sad but give us a similar lesson. The problem with this way of doing things is that those situations which do not serve us and make us feel sad can at times become burdensome to our spirit.

When you obliviously manifest a burdensome situation, it is possible that you can carry the ill-favoured creation around with you like a terrible tumour for the rest of your days. The tumour then begins to spread all over your being and you become sick with the shadow of self that you never desired to create and most certainly did not desire to become tainted with. Our immature egoic mind is fickle and troublesome. It can not be trusted in the current conditioning that it has practised for so long. It does not always know what it truly wants and when it manifests something which it does not want, it makes the entire being suffer for weeks, months, years and even, for some, lifetimes. It is therefore in the interest of the one who desires to be a master manifester to cultivate the mind in a manner which will serve their higher purpose harmoniously. The one who has nurtured their mind can bring about their heart's truest desires, without having to go through the flawed way of trial and sometimes, extremely fatal error. If you are serious about becoming a master manifester, an expert energy manipulator, you must become accustomed to the concepts of surrender and devotion.

If we are to entertain the concept of surrender as a means of reaching our truest and highest desires, we must first fully understand what is meant by the term. If we look up the term 'surrender' in the dictionary we get the definition "To stop resisting an enemy or opponent and give into their authority." This definition serves the lesson on surrendering discussed here well, and so we will use it to illustrate what is meant by surrender. To surrender, as a master manifester is to let go of the concepts of self which are causing resistance to obtaining the things you truly desire. Once you have let go of your need to control every situation from the perspective of the egoic mind, you can give the sovereignty of your life over to the divine, omnipotent authority. Why would you want to give up control of your life to something which you have never seen with your two eyes? Well, the All Conscious, all-knowing mind is far superior to the one we have created for ourselves within the human condition.

One of our hindrances to creating the life we want for ourselves without resistance is that we have made the omnipotent authority our opponent, instead of making it the core of who we are. By recognising that there is a higher authority, a conscious mind that knows more than your egoic mind can ever know, you open yourself up to receive its harmonious grace into your life. When it comes to surrendering to the omnipotent authority, it is not to say that you are to completely give up your ego or identity of self. We must have a concept of self to ground our being within so that we know how to navigate this material plane of existence. You can never completely surrender your being over to any authority, force or being without losing your ground. To completely surrender would mean to cause death to yourself and in doing so you would no longer have the awareness of being and so the pursuit of becoming a master of yourself would be utterly pointless.

The problem with surrendering to an image of God, or even to omnipotent energy, is that no matter how hard you try to let go of the person you know yourself to be, you will always find yourself back living as the person you are. You have already written a story about yourself which you use every day to navigate the world. This story tells you what and who you are so that you know what to do next; this is the role of the ego. Even 'surrendering' is a scene you are adding to your life story and depending on how much significance you give to it, surrendering can also become a programme which inhibits you from realising your highest potential.

In your practice of becoming a master manifester, you are not to give up your entire existence to a god or a higher authority. By surrendering, the master manifester is only giving up the barriers and blockages that they have created within the egoic mind, which prohibit the omnipotent authority from working through them harmoniously.

So how do we stop resisting so that we can let the greater power co-create with us? Many of the barriers of resistance created in the mind come from the ego. The egoic mind is born from the material world; the things that we can see, hear, taste, touch and feel in our immediate environment. In addition, the egoic mind is used to being in control because it provides you with physical confirmation of your immediate environment. It is within your physical environment that you feel most comfortable and therefore powerful and so through it, you strive to control it. The problem is the material world is impermanent and although it appears real, it is merely a manifestation of the soul's past yearnings and so does not confidently determine the future. Although the ego wants to be in control, really and truly the soul (which is made up of your emotions and All Consciousness) is the one in control.

If we are to remove our self-suffering, challenges and resistance while manifesting, we must surrender our means of manifesting to the soul through daily devotion. When we look in the dictionary, the first definition of devotion reads: "love, loyalty or enthusiasm for a person or activity". This definition gives full meaning to the type of devotion needed to effectively surrender to the soul while manifesting. This is why surrendering and devotion go hand in hand.

Surrendering is the conscious act of recognising that our soul has higher authority over the default dominant egoic mind, while devotion is the intentional daily practice which brings you more in tune with the pure essence and power of who you truly are. To surrender you must be in a state of devotion. Being in a state of devotion does not necessarily mean that you choose a god to worship. It also does not mean that you must constantly practise the teachings taught here in this book, even if you naturally gravitate towards doing so. Devotion in this sense is to live in a way which embodies the omnipotent power through all that you do. It is to become obsessed with being a master manifester so that you can create joy on your journey, with minimal resistance. It is to put into practice all that you have learnt here not for vanity or desperation but because you love becoming a better person and love attracting harmony into your life.

As you begin surrendering successfully, by removing the egoic programmes, you begin to realise that there is no greater way of being than to be in devotion to the spirit of balance. To dance with the supreme power which lives within all things is one of the greatest pleasures you can experience in existence.

The concept of surrendering and devotion is somewhat paradoxical and so can be tricky to embrace, however, it is also one of the more simple and effective teachings. In reality, there is no real way to practise or do a specific thing to become a devotee. To be a true devotee is to be born into a state which stops you from getting in your own way. Granted, if you continue to practise the teachings you have learnt daily your consciousness will be in the presence of the state of devotion. This is because the teachings here require you to consciously observe aspects of your soul.

When you reach the status of a true master manifester, you will come to know that you do not need anything outside of yourself to become a dedicated devotee. All you would need to be in a state of devotion is love, loyalty and enthusiasm for the process of being in your highest state of being. Understandably for the one who is striving to become a master manifester it would be beneficial to have devotional practices for training the subconscious.

For the one who has embarked on this journey, the question of 'How do I know if I'm doing it right?' may arise. This feeling may lead you to feel an obligation to perform all the teachings daily to ensure that you are 'doing it right' however, this disciplinary approach may be in vain. For the reason of consistency, here are a few ways that you can observe whether you are 'doing it right.'

Firstly, you will begin to notice that things which used to bother you no longer do. You start to become detached from your identity to self and prefer to be in blissful harmony rather than to be correct to appease your ego. For example, you may be in a conversation with someone who has challenged your perspective of self and now the situation is ripe for conflict. As a devotee, instead of becoming argumentative and feeling the urge to forcibly express your point of view, you will feel the grace of discernment to know that arguing your point will only bring resistance to the situation and therefore to yourself. Once you have observed the potential barrier to harmony that your ego may pose, you surrender your old ways of being and will look for a more compassionate way of expressing your observation of contrast in belief systems. I am not saying you will become a pushover and never feel the need to stick up for yourself however, you will prefer to feel the bliss of a harmonious situation over needing to dominate the conversation for the sake of appeasing your ego.

Another way in which you will notice that you have entered the state of devotion is that when you need to revive your spirit, you will stop turning to a substance or negative behavioural patterns but will instead naturally seek the practices given here. For example: if you have had a particularly difficult day, where your mind has not been creating in harmony with who you wish yourself to be, instead of switching on the television and indulging in a bottle of wine, you will find yourself seeking practices which allow the soul to govern. Instead of giving the ego a blanket for comfort and entertainment for distraction, the devotee will prefer to sit with their soul through meditation or through a means of releasing conflicting emotions. In doing so the devotee surrenders the manifestation of suffering that the egoic mind has created and enters a state where the omnipotent authority has the space to move through the devotee, replacing conflict with harmony.

Finally, another indication that you are in a state of devotion is by observing the nature of the thoughts that occur in your mind. It is believed that the human mind generates around eighty thousand thoughts a day and that the vast majority of these are negative and egoic. For the devotee, these negative thoughts created by the ego are an invitation for the omnipotent spirit, the All Consciousness, to come and play within the consciousness of their being. For the devotee, negative thoughts are immediately recognised as being born of the ego and not of the blissful spirit.

The devotee can recognise a negative thought like a purple cow grazing in the middle of a pigpen. This is because the devotee uses their feelings as an indication of what state they are currently in (either ego or soul). High vibrational feelings like bliss, love, laughter and contentment indicate to the devotee that the omnipotent spirit is co-creating with them. In contrast, low vibrational feelings like fear, anger, victimisation and lust indicate that the egoic mind is dominating the being and leading the devotee into a state of suffering.

The devotee knows that there is nothing wrong with having these negative thoughts and it is not the aim of the devotee to eradicate these negative thoughts entirely. They will inevitably come. The devotee's only desire when presented with the thoughts born of the ego is to allow the soul to dance with them. It is through their faith and positive visualisation that the devotee transforms negative thoughts into ones more closely aligned with the blissful vibration they ultimately dwell in.

If you are in a state of devotion, you will naturally repel negative thoughts and vibrations. You will find yourself in faith that although things may not appear to be the way you desire them to be, you know that they are becoming that which you desire; even if in ways you do not understand. To be a powerful devotee you must remove yourself from attachment to any outcome and begin trusting in your intuition. Listen to the subtle voice which twinkles in the heart and whispers to you the direction which they must take to achieve your ultimate desire harmoniously. The more you surrender over your ego by letting go of resistance, the easier it is for you to dance with the blissful spirit in a state of devotion.

At the beginning of times, there were three supreme gods who were responsible for the creation, preservation and destruction of the universe. Shiva, known for his ability to destroy aspects of creation so that new ones may be born, was married to the goddess Sati for many aeons. Shiva and Sati were inseparable. Whenever one of their names was mentioned so was the other, they could not be known without the other. Shiva loved Sati dearly and could not imagine a universe without her existence and Sati loved Shiva just as equally.

The true test of Sati's love unfolded when Daksha, Sati's father, decided to throw a spectacular celebration to honour his family and gods of virtue. This celebration is known as a Yagna. It was always common knowledge that Daksha did not approve of Sati's marriage to Shiva, for Shiva was a brute of a god. Towering in height and bulging with muscles, Shiva would darken his naked body in ash so that it mirrored dark earthly forces. His untamed warrior presence was found intimidating for most, to say the least. Daksha had begged Sati not to marry Shiva but due to their divine union and love, Sati ignored her family's wishes even though they promised to cut her off from their household.

The day of the Yagna arrived and news soon reached Sati that her father had not invited herself or her ruffian husband, Shiva, to the celebration. Disgraced by the disrespect that her father had shown to her beloved, Sati flew into the Yagna in a passionate rage. Her anger burnt so brilliantly that she set herself ablaze and soon died from the flames of her outrage. Shiva raced to the sacred ceremony after Sati but he was too late. In his distress, Shiva destroyed the ceremony and decapitated Sati's father as punishment for what he had done to her. After all the commotion Shiva, devastated by the loss of his idolised lover, retreated to the mountains where he remained in deep and unbroken meditation for uncountable days. Shiva, atop the mountain, vowed that he would remain in mourning for the rest of his days, never to marry again.

Sometime after the tragic death of Sati, Queen Menaka of the Himalayas had a vision. She dreamt that she would give birth to a daughter who would be the consort of Shiva. Having married King Himavat, who was a descendant and ruler of the Himalayan mountains, she understood Shiva's wild ways. When news reached Menaka that Sati had died, she knew that her unborn daughter would be the reincarnation of Sati and so she went into ascetic meditation to realise her desire.

In alignment with her vision and surrendering, Menaka soon gave king Himavat a beautiful baby girl who they named Uma. As king Himavat was also known as Parvatraj, they gave Uma a second name; Parvati, which means 'of the mountains'.

As soon as Parvati could walk and talk, it was very obvious that what her mother had visualised all those years ago was true as her childhood was coloured in spiritual devotion. Parvati loved spending time outdoors, collecting wildflowers and staying up late to name the stars of the ancestors in the sky. Every day she would make beautiful garlands for the gods; which were vibrantly coloured with the flowers she collected, gleefully singing Shiva's name.

The older she got, the deeper her devotion became.
She naturally gravitated towards yoga and immediately fell in love with the practice, as it gracefully allowed her to be in the presence of higher states of being. Although she was a girl, and a beautiful one at that, Parvati aspired to become a yogi so that she could free herself from the suffering of ego. Her only ambition was to become one with the flow of life, love and the universe. Parvati's father disapproved of her aspirations, for who would marry a yogi and bring honour to the family name. Despite Himavat's disapproval, Parvati wanted nothing more than to be wise like Shiva, the god of yoga. Her father's resistance only made her desire for yoga grow more intensely.

Soon Parvati was old enough to marry and her beauty and wisdom enchanted all who were aware of her existence. Marriage proposals from far, wide, noble and humble stature, surged the household of Himavat. Although she had many proposals from numerous eligible suitors, Parvati declined every single one, for how could a life of marriage replace a life of yoga. Her only focus and desires were to become one with the divine creator and she would spend every day in solitude to reach such a state if she had to. After some time, Parvati's parents began to worry whether she would ever marry. Their daughter was beautiful, wise and feminine yet she had no interest in anyone who presented themselves to her. Every time a suitor would enter their home to meet her, Parvati would rush through the formalities so that she could hurry back to her devotional practices. Parvati's parents grew tired of her lack of interest in marriage and soon tension grew in the home.

To escape the disappointed glares of her parents, Parvati began rising at the break of dawn and taking long walks to Mount Kailash so that she could peacefully perform penance until dusk arrived. Shiva, blissfully unaware of all that had been unfolding in the village below, remained in unbroken meditation and inconspicuously tucked away in the sanctuary of Kailash mountain. On one particular day, Parvati was looking for rare flowers to make her garlands when she saw the supreme Shiva sitting atop an ancient tree stump, cross-legged and eyes tightly shut. Immediately upon laying her eyes upon him, Parvati's heart skipped a beat and she fell passionately in love with Shiva. Every day Parvati would bring offerings of fresh food and elaborate garlands for Shiva. She would lay them at his feet and sing songs in his honour as a devotion of love towards him. Parvati did this every day for many years however, Shiva did not open his eyes or acknowledge her presence.

Each day that went past, Parvati fell deeper in love with Shiva and dreamed faithfully of the day that he would open his eyes and ask her to be his wife. Out in the realm of the gods, the Devas watched Parvati's desire for Shiva and were impressed by her consistent offerings and praises towards the supreme god. For many years, the absence of Shiva's participation in the god realm was causing imbalance throughout the universe. Ever since Sati's death, Shiva had lost all motivation and creative abilities to generate the destructive flow needed in both the god world and the human world. The Devas were hopeful that if Shiva only opened his eyes, he would see Parvarti and recognise her as Sati's reincarnation. They knew that once he saw his beloved, he would instantly fall in love and begin destructively creating again, restoring harmony within the universe.

The Devas grew impatient after many years of observing Parvati climb to the top of Mount Kailash to bring the dismissive Shiva offerings. They wondered if Shiva would ever open his eyes to look upon his beloved. They knew that all he had to do was open his eyes but no one dared to disturb his mourning for they knew that if they broke his meditation, Shiva would open his third eye and in a rage of anger possibly destroy the entire universe. Desperate to do something to help the persevering Parvati, the Devas went to the god Kama who was known for his ability to make anyone fall in love with the strike of his arrow. The Devas managed to convince Kama to go to Mount Kailash and shoot Shiva in the heart with his love arrow so that he would finally notice Parvati. Reluctantly, Kama made his way to Mount Kailash and waited patiently out of sight for the perfect moment to deploy the plan of the Devas.

Like clockwork, Parvati arrived at sunrise and laid floral garlands at Shiva's feet. As she was bowing to her lord, Kama took the opportunity to pull back his arrow and release it into the heart of Shiva. Shiva instantly felt a feverish heat emanate from his body as passionate love radiated throughout him. For a moment Shiva was taken aback by what he was feeling and began to open his eyes. When he realised that his meditation had been broken, Shiva was furious and sought out the culprit. Using his third eye, Shiva saw Kama hiding in the shrubbery nearby. Immediately Shiva blasted a laser beam of molten fire toward Kama, from his eye, and the Deva was incinerated on the spot. Shiva shook off his annoyance, repositioned himself and went back into deep meditation.

Parvati, having witnessed what had just happened to Kama, came to realise that lord Shiva would never acknowledge her existence in these ways. She had already spent many years bringing Shiva offerings and singing to him daily and he had not even blinked in her direction. Even the god of love had deviously attempted to alleviate Shiva from his state of mourning and that had only gotten him killed. Deep sadness took over Parvati as she realised that her sacrificial efforts would not awaken Shiva and they would not get him to marry her. Accepting defeat she chose to surrender. Parvati laid down the food and garlands that she had made for Shiva and took off her shoes and outerwear. She got down on the cold ground beside Shiva, sat cross-legged with her palms facing upward and entered a state of penance. For many months Parvati remained like this, only breaking meditation a few times to preserve her body. The light within Parvati shone brighter and brighter as the intense yoga practise allowed her to discover answers within herself which were not possible to find in the ways that she had once sought. The Deva's watched closely as the two estranged lovers flowed in yoga together yet apart. And then it happened. On that particular day when the stars were aligned, Shiva felt the most peculiar thing happen within his being. He could see a radiant light emitting from a source nearby. A light as bright as the diamond-like stars in the night sky above. Curious to know what was the source of this dazzling light, Shiva opened his eyes to see Parvati sitting beside him. She was entangled in her yoga pose, eyes closed and unaware that Shiva had awoken. At that very moment, Shiva saw Sati in Parvati and fell eternally in love with her. He vowed that he would marry the princess of the Himalayas so that she may remain by his side and become one in Kailash forevermore.

It was through ascetic yoga that Parvati realised her deepest desire which was to become one with the creator. Her desire for oneness was represented through her love and devotion to Shiva. For Parvati to achieve her manifestation, she had to let go of the ways of worship that she was used to. She had to surrender her striving to become a yogic and the wife of Shiva. Once she accepted that she was already yoga and that she was already one with the creator, her truest desire manifested. By removing the barriers that her egoic conditioning was creating, she was able to work with the divine flow and achieve all that was in her heart. Parvati is well known as the goddess of devotion because she disciplined herself and reprogrammed her mind in a way that awakened the divine within her. She allowed the harmonious spirit to flow through her that it shone brightly within her body, ultimately becoming one with it, which is symbolised through her marriage to Shiva.

The death of Kama represents the death of Parvati's egoic striving to get Shiva to look at her and love her. When she accepted there was no outside force that could make her desire for Shiva come to fruition, she surrendered her ego and devoted herself to the mind of oneness, the All Consciousness.

Although Sati achieved her desires through surrendering, it is not to say that her daily offerings and passion for spiritual practices were in vain. These disciplines were the stepping stones that led Parvati to the river of purification. As the ego dominates the human condition for the majority of people, to become a master of your world, it is necessary to start thinking in the ways of goddess Parvati. To be a master manifester you must surrender your ego and allow yourself to become more fluid, flexible and detached from the expectations of the ego. Once you become devoted to the secrets which nest peacefully within your being, you will become open to the flow of the divine, allowing it to creatively flow through you and manifest your truest desires.

12 ALCHEMY

Whenever alchemy is mentioned, most people's minds automatically turn to think about the infamous alchemists of the 15th century who spent many days leaning over bunsen burners, attempting to turn lead into gold. Although learning the ability to transform a fairly inexpensive base metal like lead into a much more globally valued noble metal like gold would surely meet the desires of many, it is not what we are going to be learning here. Although it might be cool to know how to perform such wizardry, let's be reminded that mercury poisoning was the fatal fate for many of the aspiring alchemists who wished to realise their fortune through the means of physical transmutation. The alchemy that is to be shared here in this chapter is a lot safer to practise and arguably more effective at bringing about one's most desired manifestations.

The meaning of Alchemy is to transform or transmute one state of being/matter into another, through a process of mixing the original state with an 'elixir' until it becomes the new desired state. For the alchemists of the 15th century, an elixir was some kind of philosopher's stone or magical substance that they could add to their experiments and produce the thing they most desire, gold. Many alchemists spent the majority of their careers seeking out the magical stone or powder which would produce their desires but to no avail. For the master manifester, however, the magical substance that is used to transmute the physical world around you is that found in your own human imagination.

Our brain is made of thousands of chemicals, many of which even the greatest scientist do not yet fully understand. When these chemicals of the brain are mixed with the right amount of mental imagery, human emotion and natural laws, the master manifester possesses the ability to transform physical matter into a new desired state. With the right balance of chemicals and emotions within the human being, it is possible to create a tangible manifestation. The principles of alchemy shared here are to the master manifester, the golden goose whose eggs can forever be transformed into gold.

A brief history of the concept of alchemy is important for the student of the master's work to understand so that they can use the techniques listed herein successfully. The term alchemy is believed to have originated in ancient Egypt, the etymology of which can be broken down into two parts: Al, meaning the divine or of the divine (e.g Allah) and Khem, meaning 'black' or dark matter which pertains to the people occupying ancient Egypt at the time. Khem is also where the term chemistry comes from, which in modern terms is the study of elements of which matter is composed. When we put the terms together to produce 'alchemy' it can literally be interpreted as black magic. Now do not fear. Yes, the term black magic has many negative connotations related to it however, in alchemy the term means a divine intervention over matter which is born out of the darkness/the formless. Once the student latches on to this concept, they can continue the study of the master's work without fear or scepticism. To get to the point without dwelling on the actual meaning of the term alchemy, the master's work as it relates to alchemy is to turn darkness into light; to turn the less desirable into the most desirable.

The aspiring alchemists of the 15th century, may not have understood everything to do with the process of transmutation but they did understand, at least, that alchemy is a process of purification. They understood that the base metal they were working with, already contained within it the properties to become the noble metal which they desired. When the alchemist held the lead in his hands, he knew that the only thing keeping him apart from the gold that he desired, was the impurities tainting the lead he was currently working on. Through the process of transmutation, the alchemist purifies the undesirable state. Once the threshold of purification has been reached, the state which he desires most appears before him. The aspiring alchemists also understood that to be able to purify the lead, something had to be added to it so that a gradual purging process could take place and as a result produce the gold he desired.

Although gold can be manifested through the process of alchemy, it is not the highest order for practising such ancient arts. The highest order of alchemy is the transmutation and purification of matter through consciousness. In previous chapters, we have established that we are floating in a sea of conscious thought. This sea of conscious thought is divine and contains everything and anything that has and could be imagined. You are very much a part of that conscious thought and in your sovereignty have access to any and all of the thoughts contained within the all-knowing sea of consciousness. The only obstacle is that your human condition is plagued with impurities which deny you access to certain aspects of the All Consciousness. These include your fears, anxiety, self-doubt, false programmes and just pure ignorance of the power which lay dormant for most in the collective human consciousness.

If you wish to do the master's work, if you wish to know how to manipulate the material world in your favour, you must first be in a process of self-purification. Before you will have any chance of success, you the student must be in the process of transforming the darkness within you into light. This is the highest order, for when you become the master of the light within yourself, you become the master of all in this life and lives beyond.

The ignorant alchemist who was in search of gold used alchemy for a lower order. He spent decades of his life looking for an elixir or philosopher's stone to bring light to the dark, impure base metal that contained within its imperfections his riches. What he failed to notice is that the light he sought within the elixir was already within him. This is not some hocus pocus fanciful thinking statement that I make here. This is a simple observation that anyone can make and that we have already made together at least once. Just in case you missed it, let's observe the light within you again. What have you eaten today? Let's just say for demonstration it was a banana. When you ate that banana where did it go? Of course, some of it passes through your digestive system but for the most part, that banana was transformed from a fruit into a human being. What you ate earlier has become a part of your cells and is contributing to your ongoing life. Now how did that banana become you? Think about this for a moment. We could get into all the scientifics about the wonders of the human digestive system but that is not going to help us here. The principle remains that there is an automatic process within you, a divine intelligence, that through its striving to sustain your life, transforms the banana (matter) into life force energy which keeps your heart beating. The transformation was done by the light within you.

At the same time as saying that it was done by the divine light within you, was it not also you who performed this transmutation of banana into a human being? Subtle yet profound observation. The more you remove the heaviness of dark matter which makes up your being, the closer you come to understanding the light which exists within you. The closeness comes by becoming. You have to become the light to know how to work from it. So how can you become the light? How is it that you can purify yourself in such a way that the material realm becomes like putty for you to mould in whatever way you most desire?

To begin, every alchemist needs a laboratory; a safe place where you can do the work of purification. I'm not saying that you transform your kitchen into a science experiment however, if you are aspiring to become a master manifester it is mandatory that you get your life in order. You must be able to have a space within yourself where you can retreat peacefully and work with the light which has been disguised by angles and shadows. Once you have found this place, work can begin. To build such a place for yourself, it is vital to practice techniques such as meditation. Meditation is a fantastic way to clear space so that the light within can come to be recognised within your consciousness.

Once the laboratory has been established and the light is visibly burning on the bunsen within, you can begin to work with the light under the seven natural laws. These natural laws are principle states which act as the elements in the periodic table for the master. These natural laws consist of the following:

(1) All is one and one is all
(2) Everything is energy and everything vibrates
(3) Everything has a correspondence
(4) Everything has a gender
(5) All things exist on a pole from negative to positive
(6) Every effect has a cause, and finally
(7) There is a cyclic rhythm which all things dance to in the universe.

Before going into detail about these seven natural laws let's first understand that the seven laws can correspond to the seven masters of the emerald tablets, the seven hermetic principles and also the seven chakras. As above, so below. If our seven chakras are not sufficiently aligned, then it will be pointless to even try to make the seven laws work for us. In contrast, if we are in perfect harmony within ourselves then the seven laws will work innately for us. To be a master manifester, you will want to know how to possess power over these laws rather than just having them function by default. Before working with any of these laws always remember to have the light within turned on.

The first law, All is one and one is all, refers to the commonly overlooked principle that all which exists has come from the same conscious mind. Some religious people would argue that everything came from god however the god that they speak of and the law of one described here are not directly related. The god of religion has been born out of the All but is not it in principle. We have attempted to describe the All Consciousness several times but its complete nature is a phenomenon which can never be fully known. The best way to describe the All One is to picture an ocean that expands across all corners of the universe and fills all space. It knows no time yet is forever flowing. It permeates all aspects of life and makes up everything. Even when you cry, you cry tears made up of oceanic salt water. Every living thing swims within the ocean of the All. Every movement, gesture or shiver causes ripples and waves within the endless ocean that are felt by everyone. The ocean of consciousness is the womb of creation where all forms are born, yet it is also the energetic force which allows forms to be held together and supported. It is everything, yet it is no-thing. It is the cause of all individuals yet can not be personified as an objective being.

Once you understand this principle you begin to see the true underlying nature of forms and you recognise that all forms you observe are not separate from yourself. All forms are but an extension of yourself within the All One. Through the recognition of energy types and the purifying of self, the veil is removed and the master manifester has the opportunity to transmute a form into whatever it is he likes.

Law 2 is Vibration. The principle of vibration simply put is the recognition that everything moves, everything is energy and everything carries a certain frequency. Even the most inanimate looking object is vibrating to some degree. Even the things which we can not perceive around us are vibrating, however, they are moving at frequencies which we can not pick up on within the limitations of our five human senses.

You may or may not remember being taught that energy can never die, it can only ever be transformed. $E=MC^2$ is one of the world's most famous equations and breaks the fundamental meaning of this principle down. It illustrates that energy, light and matter are interchangeable. When one moves into a new state, so do the others. With this being understood, the master manifester knows that by simply changing the frequency at which something vibrates he can also change its appearance into a new state. Similarly, he understands that by changing something's appearance, whether physically or within his mind's eye, he can change its frequency. By increasing the amount of light illuminating from a material object, the master manifester can manipulate that object's frequency so that it matches the frequency of the desired state. The light needed to transform the object of attention can be harnessed from the formless shadow/the void residing within the manifester. This light will be known to the manifester once he has purged himself of impurities so that he matches the vibration of the desired state.

Law 3 is Correspondence. In this principle, the master manifester understands that what occurs in the outer world is a direct reflection of what is occurring within his inner world. As above, so below. As below, so above. With this knowledge, the master manifester knows that he is constantly projecting his ideas and state of being onto the material world around him. It is his attention to things and his awareness of their relation to himself, which gives him the ability to transmute physical material into a form of matter which most reflects his desired vision. For example, I was recently watching an interview with abstract graffiti artist Basquiat from 1983. In that interview, he tells the journalist that he was in hindsight glad that he was rejected from a fine art school because the refined techniques and theorised learning would have taken away from the essence of who he was as an artist. The absence of fine art school allowed him to learn techniques which earned him millions of dollars because he spent time around other expressive and creative artists. Basquiat transmuted his seemingly negative experience of rejection for a desirable contribution to his unconventional success.

Basquiat was fully empowered by his vision to succeed as a famous artist, that he let the light from his vision inspire him to act on his environment. He transformed his environment so that it reflected the vision of success he held within his mind's eye. He literally painted on the street walls of New York and signed them by his pen name, Samo, so that his outside environment became who he believed himself to be, internally. All can perform this alchemy for all are one with this principle of correspondence. Hold your vision so firmly in your mind so that everything, even the seemingly counterintuitive things, act in a way that brings about the vision of who you believe yourself to be. When done correctly, inspiration, intuition, people, conversations and newly acquired skills will begin to flow into your experience in a way that projects the correspondence from within onto the material realm.

Law 4 is Gender. The law of gender exists not only in this realm but in realms beyond our human comprehension. It is a divine order which gives interpretation as to how things are created into form. We can see gender in so many aspects of the physical and abstract world. For example, a flower possesses both male and female parts which carry either the pollen or the space for incubation where new plants come into existence (i.e the womb).

In most latin laced languages, there are words which are feminine and words which are masculine. This is in recognition that certain objects, forms and energies carry either a male or female principle. We even describe our abstract world in terms of the feminine and the masculine. For example, we speak of mother earth as being the life force which sustains and nurtures our existence. We also talk of our father God, the omnipotent consciousness that wills things into existence. Recognising how these dual principles work and how they exist within and around us is of great importance to the master manifester. All things in creation have a male or female counterpart. For the master manifester, he knows that once he knows the gender of the matter he is currently observing, he can match its energy with either its male or female counterpart to give birth to his desired creation. If the master manifester, for example, is wanting to sell some products online he may first devise the entire business plan. He may then produce a great marketing strategy and brand the products so that they are perfectly coherent. These are all nurturing feminine aspects. He recognises however that to actually produce a successful business, he must invest money into the products by purchasing them. He must then put the products on an online platform to sell and then actively will the sale of those products by putting them into the attention of the consumer through advertising. This activity is the masculine aspect. Both combined in a harmonious way will create a selling success.

Law 5 is the law of Polarity. Polarity may be one of the most profound laws to digest yet it is as simple as this. There is a duality in everything. If there is hot, there is cold. If it is dark, there is also light. When there is love, there is also hate. When we say that we hate something we can also say that we do not love it as much as we love something else. In this sense, hate does not exist only as a concept of itself. Hate is love only it exists as the polar opposite of pure love. As we move down the pole of love we meet like, indifferent, dislike and finally hate. For the master manifester, to recognise this is to recognise the potentiality to transform one existing state into its polar opposite using the power of transmutation. For example, If the master manifester were to look around him and see objects which reflected a state of poverty, he could use his understanding of polarity to realise that the poverty he perceives is only another form of wealth. The fact that he can perceive poverty means that within him lies a vibration of vast wealth that allows him to view such a contrast. Using his light, the master manifester can transmute those objects into the wealth he wishes to see by visualising them as becoming their polar opposite. He may for example see a basic and broken clock hanging on the wall. He can then visualise its vibrational enhancement by replacing it with the image of a luxurious and professionally crafted clock ticking away harmoniously in his mind's eye. The master manifester can do this with almost anything including his feelings. If he feels sad, firstly he can recognise that sadness exists on the same pole as happiness. Next, he can explore the reason why he is sad and transmute its cause into an effect of happiness by replacing those sad thoughts with ones slightly brighter and brighter and brighter still, until finally happiness is his reality.

Law 6 is Causation. This law simply states that every cause has its effect. We have already gone into great detail about the principle of cause and effect in a previous chapter so for ease of reading I will not repeat it here. If you have not yet embarked on this chapter, the master manifester uses the law of causation to acknowledge that all things manifested are an effect of something that caused its existence. Nothing is left untouched by this principle, like all the principles. Using this knowledge, the master manifester uses his mind's eye and willpower to become the cause of the effect he wishes to see. He uses the present moment to visualise his desires, while also acting on the present manifested effects so that they become the cause of his desired state.

Law 7 is Rhythm. The law of rhythm is the recognition that all phenomena occur in a harmonious symphony made up of high and low cycles. Just as things rise, they also fall. What goes up must come down for this is the rhythmic consequence of the harmonious song we are all a part of.

For the master manifester, rhythm is a natural part of life. He does not feel fear in a cycle of a low vibratory nature for he knows that his descending is a necessary factor towards his ascendence. In fact, for the one who begins the master's work, he may find that once he has made progress in his understanding of these concepts and begins to integrate them into his own life, the material world appears to collapse around him. Many cycles in his life will come to an end and concepts he once believed will come to challenge his conscious mind.

In the beginning, it will be an intense period of self-purging. A stormy sonata made up of crashing cymbals and tense drums. As sure as the crescendo of challenges peaks at the pole of seemingly impossible circumstances, the material world around the master manifester orchestrates itself in a way which begins to reflect his purified internal state. The harmonies slow down to an ethereal hum of just a few string instruments, giving him subtle confirmation of where the next cycle of events is taking him. The playful chirps of a friendly flute begin a momentum towards the manifesters desired state and he dances with delight knowing he is becoming. Even in the master manifester's winter seasons, when the leaves are falling from the trees and it seems as if he has been buried, he is not swayed. He neutralises the cold of the winter by transmuting it into the warm desired state emerging from his subconscious. He performs this neutralisation by changing the thought process of his conscious mind to one which is in recognition of the law of rhythm. Instead of seeing himself as buried in the depths of despair, he sees himself as but a seed which has been planted in the fall and waits patiently for the freshness that spring brings. When spring arrives, as it always does, the master manifester will blossom in this cycle of rebirth until his fruits are ripe and abundant at the height of summer.

In 3384 BC Enoch, the son of Jared was born. Enoch was a just man who walked with god for all the days of his life. Through his spiritual perfection, Enoch's eyes were open to the secrets of god, secrets which had been hidden from the average man. He would often have vivid visions of heavenly worlds and converse with spirits of higher planes. Many of the visions he did not share with others for they merely would not understand. He did, however, have one vision in particular which gave a prophecy for the benefit of future generations. He named this generation the Watchers and their Giants. In his vision, Enoch prophecies that the Watchers will all come to know the mighty power of God. For some, this power will cripple them and become a curse but for others, the power of God will become a great blessing to their lives. Here lies the prophecy of Enoch.

In ancient times, man was not much more sophisticated than the animals and beasts they walked among. Although primitive in nature, there was something about the heart of man that captured the attention of angelic beings whose residence was in heaven. It was the women of man in particular who caught the attention of these heavenly spirits, for their hearts radiated with loving desire and magnetic longing. Seduced by their beauty, the angels conspired among themselves and decided that they would each take a human wife and sleep with her so that she would give birth to children who were half human and half angelic.

Semjaza was the leader of the angels and feared that the other angels would go back on their decision if he was to be the first to perform such an unheard-of act. The other angels however agreed to take an oath so that they were bound by a curse to perform the act. Led by Semjaza and eighteen superior angels, two hundred heavenly spirits went to earth and slept with the daughters of man. The women soon became pregnant and after a while gave birth to giants who were great in stature. The giants became dominant on earth and devoured all the things which man had created out of nature. They took over every system, every way of being and every corner of the earth until mankind could no longer provide for himself in the way that he always had. Soon the earth was almost unrecognisable for what the daughters of man and fallen angels had given birth to. The giants, which dominated the earth, began to sin against the birds, animals and insects that man had once protected. Soon after, the earth became sick resulting in natural disasters and deathly diseases among mankind.

Though the sons of the fallen angels had caused so much destruction on earth, it was not their presence in mankind which was the greatest sin. Some of the fallen angels, who now resided on earth, began to teach man heavenly wisdom. The secrets which they disclosed were reserved for the holy ones who resided in heaven and were not intended for mankind at his stage of evolution. The fallen angel Azazel, in particular, taught mankind about vanity and warfare. With these secret skills, man learned how to manipulate the substances on the earth so that he could create any vision of his imagination. Other fallen angels taught mankind about astrology and the energies of the earth, which some used to cast spells and other forms of energy manipulation. After some time, fornication and wickedness plagued the earth. Rather than his evolution, the insight of supreme knowledge brought destruction onto man so that their cries could be heard from heaven.

The archangels Michael, Gabriel, Surjan and Urjan heard the cries of humanity and organised a council between them and the great Lord. They spoke of the sins which Azazel had unleashed onto the earth and of the giants which had devoured the ways of man. It was clear that a resolution was needed to save humanity from its downfall. The most high and holy one heard the concerns of the archangels and agreed that harmony should be restored on earth. Through his prophet, Noah, the Lord spoke. Noah prophesied that a great flood would come and cleanse the earth of Azazel's sins. Although many men were tainted by the mysteries that the fallen angels had disclosed to them, Noah told all who would listen that not all of man would be destroyed by the disclosed holy wisdom. Those who were just would survive.

Azazel, however, would be cast into darkness for eternity so that he would never know light again. As for the sons of the fallen angels, the bastards who were full of lust and oppression, they would destroy each other through murder so that their days would come to an end without knowing eternal life. The rest of the fallen angels, including Semjaza, would be taken to the ends of the earth for seventy generations before burning in the destructive flames of the abyss. With their incineration, the souls of lust, oppression and the children of the fallen angels would be destroyed. Wickedness would be replaced by justice and righteousness and therefore the burden of the hidden wisdom would be transformed into a blessing and a source of joy for the children of men. Trees of desire would grow on earth, bearing fruits of abundance and never again would a flood be cast on earth.

While in a state of meditation, Enoch again entered the astral planes, where he met with the great holy one in confidence. When the great holy one's voice came to him he heard it command him to ask the fallen angels why they had gone to the earth to act like men. Why had they taken women and created giants as sons when once they were holy, eternal and spiritual beings who were beyond the 3D limitations of man? The giants, which angels and man had created, had been manifested from the spiritual plane into the material one, a power previously reserved only for God. The giants were deemed as evil as they had taken on a life of their own and caused destruction on earth. They never eat any food or drink any wine because their character is invisible. There would never be a time that the giants would rise against man as it is from man which they are born. However, the fallen angels, who were once holy and in heaven would be bound to earth until the day of judgement.

Once Enoch delivered this message to the earth dwellers, he was again taken into another dimension of heaven, this time by the angel Rafael. On his travels, he saw magnificent mountain terrain with four valleys of land beneath them, covered in land beautiful enough for angels to live in. Enoch asked Rafael about these places and Rafael explained that each place had its purpose. One place, which had a spring of water and light above it, had been made for the souls who were just in their separation from the spirit world. The other places were made for the souls who died on earth without judgement. These souls were deemed as sinners who not only sinned but had not entered judgement, therefore their souls would remain bound to the earth for eternity, for they were complete in their crimes.

Again, Enoch ventured through the outer plane of existence with the angels and saw great paradisical trees, which were splendid in their fragrance. When Enoch questioned why these holy trees' perfumes resembled frankincense and myrrh, the angels replied to him that these were trees reserved for the judgement of the just. They also explained that those trees which barred fruit similar to the aloe and almond trees were the same trees that his forefather Adam and mother Eve had eaten from to obtain wisdom. Beyond the splendour, the heavenly party also passed valleys covered in hard rocks and sharding crystals. When Enoch asked what these places were for, the angels replied that they had been reserved for people who never sought to know the wisdom of the infinite.

Like most true alchemists, little is known about the life and activities of Enoch. A few elusive passages in religious texts claim that he fathered two children and that *"He walked with God. And he was no more for God took him."* Before these passages were documented, stating that "God took him" it was understood at the time that Enoch spent 365 years on earth moving in the mysterious ways of the master, before disappearing from the face of the earth without a trace. No funeral was held for him and no resting place was announced for his departure. This is because Enoch did not die. It is known by those who seek the mysteries of the infinite, that Enoch had reached a certain level of perfection in his journey to mystic mastery that he became immortal. He has indeed achieved the obtention of the philosopher's stone or the elixir of life that so many alchemists who preceded him spent numerous days in vain pursuit.

Needless to say, the process of how to become a full alchemic master was disclosed only to a few in secrecy and through hidden symbolism. This is because he who obtained the power of perfection and immortality possessed the power of a god. Like many alchemists, Enoch knew that having the power to be able to manifest almost anything at godly will, was not something to be disclosed to the general public and certainly not to those who had not yet reached a certain level of purification. Although Enoch did not want the secrets of manifestation mastery to get into the wrong hands, he did want to help those seekers of their higher power to have some sort of support on their journey.

The book of Enoch/Giants is all about manifesting. The key message to take away from this passage of highly saturated symbolism is that there is more than one dimension and more than one place of existence. The life that we create here on earth also affects the life that we create in the spiritual realm. This is because the seven laws stated above transgress that of the All Consciousness/ the holy one that Enoch talks of. These laws exist in all space and time and are symbolised in the story above as mountains, angels and ages.

The giants, which were born as the sons of the fallen angels and man are not to be mistaken for actual mythical, gigantic beings. Remember in the end, they were described as invisible manifestations which do not take food or drink. Although they are not mythical beings of great stature, they are the things which man, through his spiritual marrying to greater wisdom, has created on earth. Without the knowledge of astrology, numbers or how to weld metal, man would not have known how to build giants such as the Empire State building or the great pyramids. Without the wisdom of the fallen angels, man would not know how to use metal to create machine guns which kill, or petrol cars which cause pollution. These physical manifestations are the giants born of man. They are the things which through our desire, we manifest onto the physical plane. It is our god-like desire which gives life to manifestations which are god-like. The significance of desire is symbolised here by the fallen angels marrying the daughters of man. Remember in previous chapters that desire is a feminine principle. Women, in these passages, are used as a symbol to give light to the concept of a god-like desire needed when manifesting into the material plane.

The fallen angels, or the Watchers, represent ourselves who once, in an alternate dimension and alternative state of being, lived a spiritual life where everything was as one. Because everything was as one, there was no need for desires to manifest anything as everything was already readily available and in a state of harmonic bliss. In this 3D reality, however, we dwell in a state of perceived separation. This is a state which takes us away from the divine. We are fallen angels, separated from our divinity so that we can be watchers of conscious thought manifesting into the 3D reality of earth. This separation allows us to learn lessons about how to become a master manifester. Perceived separation from the All Consciousness also teaches us who we are as spiritual light beings as we take the time to learn everything that we are not.

When you are willing to master these lessons, the heavens are laid at your feet and your desires will bloom on trees that bear fruit of abundance. Hellish problems occur, however only for those people who neglect their call to mastery and never turn their hearts to the necessary purging and cleansing needed to transform back to their true selves. When a person does not judge their false programmes, life lessons and the truth of what is felt in their heart, their soul becomes heavy with dark matter and they become bound to the earth because they have forgotten their true heavenly nature. Remember who you are. You are a powerful light being who has come to this earth to master manifestation. You are a spiritual light being of great magnitude and beauty, living a human existence. Through continuous striving to create, you are learning about the true nature of the infinite. Through the willingness to let go of paradigms and programmes that no longer serve you, you are learning about the true nature of the soul. The more you learn and purge, the cleaner your heart becomes. This cleansing through purging allows your spirit to be lighter to the point where your manifestations become seamless, blissful and god-like. May you forever dream a dream of great wonder and may you always have the courage to become that which gives your heart life, so that you may always manifest like a god.

ABOUT THE AUTHOR

Lorae Knight is a spiritual student and self-proclaimed interdimensional dweller. Some of her earliest memories were folding up A4 sheets of paper, stapling the brim together and writing novels for children. This debut book, therefore, is a manifestation of a dream she has carried since a young age. This book is dedicated to her nine-year-old self.

Lorae has a psychology degree from the University of Essex which complements the comprehensive deep dives in her writing. Lorae has a heritage in Jamaica but was born and raised in the South East of England. She is a mother to a star seed child, born under a constellation with nine points.

Lorae enjoys the arts and music, she also has an interest in tech which provides her with the platform to exercise her brainpower.

Becoming a single mother unexpectedly sparked a heroic journey of the heart for Lorae, a journey which awakened her to many truths. This book in particular was prophesied to be written by Lorae some weeks before she became pregnant with her first child. In the vision, she was seen sitting on the ground writing a tale with words she did not know yet. After the vision she said to herself aloud "I don't want to be sat at home just to look after a baby" Yet it was a destiny she would have to undertake in order to heal the masculine, purify herself and finally manifest the dreams she has written.

Made in the USA
Columbia, SC
20 October 2022